PAUL! MAY I SPEAK WITH YOU?

**Six Dialogues
For Bible Study**

BY MARION FAIRMAN

C.S.S. Publishing Co., Inc.
Lima, Ohio

PAUL! MAY I SPEAK WITH YOU?

Copyright © 1993 by
The C.S.S. Publishing Company, Inc.
Lima, Ohio

Library of Congress Cataloging-in-Publication Data

Fairman, Marion.
    Paul! May I speak with you? : six dialogues for Bible study / by Marion Fairman.
    115 p.   14 by 21.5 cm.
    ISBN 1-55673-601-1
    1. Paul, the Apostle, Saint — Study and teaching — Textbooks. I. Title.
BS2507.F35   1993
225.9'2—dc20   92-40072
                                                                              CIP

9321 / ISBN 1-55673-601-0

To my husband who, through our love
for each other and our mutual faith in
Christ, has become one with me.

Table Of Contents

Preface

Several years ago at a missionary conference, one of the speakers laughingly referred to the Apostle Paul as his "model" — a person who often failed to "get along" with fellow workers, one who publicly challenged Peter over his "double-talk," one who adamantly refused to take John Mark on the second missionary journey. My sense of shock at his words brought home how seldom I thought of biblical characters as "real people."

As a child I never saw Christ portrayed in a pageant or a play except as a spotlight, a white robe thrown across a chair, a shadow or a voice from the wings. The humanity of Jesus seemed not to be there for me to see but always just coming on stage or just going off. Often, even today, we can hear a hint of that same unconscious denial of Jesus as "fully human." At the name of Jesus, the voice goes careful, the tone pontifical and a paralysis creeps into the dialogue.

This curious attitude toward the person of Christ has spread to his disciples, his friends and believers. My purpose in these dialogues has been to chisel away the unreality grown up about "Saint Paul."

The details of the "human" Paul are tucked away in scattered portions of scripture; other kinds of detail may be hidden in secular events of which we are largely ignorant. It seems fitting to have Paul "interviewed" by a modern woman who knows little about him excepting she is pretty sure he did not "like" women.

Paul's life-line looks like a map tracing a series of journeys: from Tarsus, his birth place, to Jerusalem — and study with Gamaliel; from Jerusalem through his crisis conversion to Damascus — and Christians he had plotted to destroy; from Damascus, through the Arabian desert, to Jerusalem — and isolation from both Christians and Jews. Hustled out of Jerusalem, he marked time in Tarsus until Barnabas came and took him to Antioch where he finally found acceptance.

Out of Antioch came Paul on those three incredible journeys to Cyprus and Asia Minor and Europe where he developed his manner of mission, methods still studied and discussed today. And then that last perilous sail to Rome — where he would die. All of these many journeys form a pattern of "breakthrough" not only in Paul's outward life but in his inner. Light strikes him down on the Damascus road and he is left blind. This proud man led into Damascus waits in darkness until he is "ready" for Ananias to restore his sight. On the Damascus road Paul has experienced the death of pride, ego and very self. And he has believed in the risen Christ (impossible except in the presence of the Eternal God). Still, he is blind. Perhaps only when a person recognizes his own helplessness and exhibits a willingness to ask for help does there occur a "bursting" of that which imprisons.

Paul was often stubborn and abrasive and arrogant. Perhaps his sufferings, his imprisonments, his desertion by friends, effect in his inner life such "breakthroughs," all the while he obediently continues on his geographical journeys. In any case, in his faith-journey, Paul, a real human being, experiences, time after time, that precious "freedom in Christ."

Suggestions For The Teacher

Suggested Uses

1. As a weekly series of Bible study for senior highs, college students, young adults and adults in the church school.
2. For any group of persons who come together, weekly or monthly, to study the Bible.
3. As a six-week series of dialogue-sermons in the worship hour of the church.
4. For older children in a vacation Bible school, a youth fellowship or a summer camp. To be used on a daily or weekly basis and coordinated with craft and other projects concerning Paul's life.

Possible Projects

1. Prepare a large line map and trace Paul's movements, adding to the map each session. Use different colors for the many places he lived and for each of his missionary journeys.
2. Using an atlas, allow children to take turns locating all of the places mentioned by Paul.
3. Mark a modern map of the area to show those places mentioned by Paul still existing under a modern name.
4. Using a modern map, calculate the miles Paul covered in his journeys.
5. Write a paper describing Paul as a person.
6. Draw a book of sketches of transportation means in Paul's day.
7. Draw a book of sketches of clothes worn in the first century by Mediterranean peoples.
8. Paint a picture of some striking scene from each dialogue — the stoning of Stephen, Paul's conversion experience, the escape in the basket from Damascus, the shipwreck at Malta; the bite of the snake, the burning of Rome, the martyrdom of Paul.

Suggested Preparations

1. No need exists to memorize the dialogue; they may be given in the mode of readers' theater. The participants should, however, practice the scripts until dramatic reality is achieved.

2. A woman is suggested as the partner to Paul in the dialogues because of the pleasing differences in voices. If desired, however, a man may take this part. In that case, be sure the voices are different, each distinctive in tone, timbre and volume.

3. Keep the physical set-up simple. Perhaps place two stools for good visibility and two music stands to hold the scripts. The stools may be positioned about five or six feet apart, turned slightly toward each other. If desired, a simple backdrop or screen may be placed behind the participants.

4. If it is difficult to hear in the room, each person should use a microphone, either a lavalier or a standing mike. A standing microphone should not block the faces of the participants.

5. If desired, use spotlights on the two speakers. Good general lighting, however, will work well.

Suggested Costumes

1. The woman speaking to Paul (or the man) may wear 20th century clothing suitable to the group and the occasion.

2. The Apostle Paul may wear a robe of any color, preferably a light color, a long robe with full sleeves. Over this robe he may wear a loose tunic, knee length, preferably a striped material. Blouse the tunic with a sash. For Paul's head, you may cover a scullcap shell with black felt and trim it with gold braid. For variety during the six sessions of dialogue, you may drape a large square of white, cream or wheat-colored cheesecloth around his head and shoulders. He may wear a chin beard. Both the scullcap shell and the chin beard may be found at a costume shop. To suggest an outdoor Paul in some dialogues, you may drape a darker or heavier piece of

material around one shoulder and let it hang down. He should wear sandals. No socks, no jewelry; check especially for a wrist watch. You will discover other ideas for costuming Paul by studying library books of biblical costumes.

Suggested Procedures

1. The class or group may be led by one or both of the participants in the dialogues, or by a third person.

2. As people gather, pass out the scripture references for each session so they may refer to it as the dialogue proceeds or check for accuracy and study later on.

3. Open the first session by giving a historical background for the first century, and by distributing, in addition to the scripture references, the list of secular events that help to establish the dates for Paul's life. (See materials.)

4. After each dialogue, if desired, pass out the questions (in materials) to direct the discussion. If the group is knowledgeable, the questions may not be necessary.

5. The leader may wish to use a flip-chart or a blackboard to build on developing ideas from each dialogue.

6. In each discussion, determine the relevance of what has been discussed in the dialogue to the individual Christian's life and to the work of the church in the 20th century.

7. In the final session, discuss those things discovered in the totality of the dialogues. Draw out what was new to group members, what they found to be of value to their lives, and those things that may be instructive to the work of the church.

8. Each dialogue takes about 20 minutes. The Apostle Paul should exit after the dialogue. If he is to take part in the discussion he may reenter as himself, that is, the person playing the part of Paul.

11

Historical Background

**The Historical Background Of The
Jewish-Greek-Roman World Of The First Century**
When the walls of Jerusalem were breached in July, 587
B.C., during the siege of Nebuchadnezzar, many Jews were
exiled to Babylon, an event marking the beginning of the dis-
persion of the Jews. In this exile and later ones, the scattered
Jews held onto their faith; many devoted themselves to the
study and practice of the Law. The edict of Cyrus (538 B.C.)
allowed the exiles to return to Jerusalem to rebuild the temples. Only a portion of the exiles returned, however, making
the dichotomy between Palestinian Jews and Jews of the *Diaspora.*

The Greeks, unified under Alexander, defeated the Persians in several important battles. In 331, Alexander founded
the great city of Alexandria and returned to the north where
he inflicted a final defeat on the Persians at Arabela. He
returned to Babylon where he died in 323. He had forged a
vast empire.

With Alexander's death, the Jews, for more than 100 years,
fell under the control of the Ptolemaic dynasty. The large number of Jews living out of Palestine, especially in Alexandria,
created a need for the translation of the Old Testament into
Greek, marking the process of Hellenization of the scattered
Jews.

At the same time, in Palestine, the fundamental nature of
the Jewish community remained unchanged; primarily it was
a religious association, headed by a high priest who combined
civil and religious authority in his own person. The Jews of
Palestine maintained only loose ties with the Hellenized Jews
living throughout the Mediterranean, seeing themselves sepa-
rated from all nations, chosen by God to survive the disaster
of the *Diaspora* and to reconstitute the people of God.

In 200 B.C. when the Seleucid King, Antiochus, defeated
the troops of Ptolemy V at Panion, Palestine passed from

13

the Ptolemaic to the Seleucid aegis. Antiochus' policy was one of unity (therefore the Hellenization of all his subjects) and of expansion which meant the appropriation of large sums of money from the Jews. The Jews of Palestine rallied to the Maccabee family as Antiochus' repressive measures increased; in 167 they issued the summons to revolt. Judas Maccabeus whipped into shape a guerilla force whom he led into a succession of incredible victories against the forces of Antiochus IV. Antiochus settled for a treaty giving the Jews of Palestine the right to follow their own laws.

The Hellenistic Jews, however, opposed Judas Maccabeus and sought protection against him from the new King Demetrius I. Demetrius appointed their candidate, Alcimus, to the high priesthood. The split among the Jews was never so clear as at this point.

Under a succession of Maccabean and Hasmonean rulers, war raged between Palestine and surrounding countries. Finally, Aristobulus became king and high priest of Judea. He was immediately opposed by Hyrcanus, supported by Aretas, King of the Nabetans. The Nabetans marched into Judea and locked Aristobulus in Jerusalem.

Rome intervened in the dispute, moving Pompey into Damascus in 63 and finally into Jerusalem. There, Pompey imprisoned Aristobulus, accepting Hyrcanus as high priest. Palestine became part of the Roman province of Syria. The 100 years of independence won for the Palestine Jews by the Maccabee family came to a bitter end.

In 49 B.C., when Julius Caesar crossed the Rubicon, his rival, Pompey, withdrew his troops to the East. With Pompey's defeat in the Egyptian delta (48), Hyrcanus quickly shifted his allegiance to Caesar. Caesar arrived in Syria in 47. He rewarded Hyrcanus by confirming his high priesthood; Hyrcanus' friend, Antipater, became prefect of Judea; two of his sons were appointed governors — Phasael over Jerusalem, Herod over Galilee. The next years were marked by the continual intrigues of Jewish leaders trying to win or preserve the favor of the Roman governors.

14

During all these political maneuverings, Herod managed to survive. He gained the favor of Mark Antony who declared him King of Judea. Still, Herod had to conquer his kingdom, which, with the aid of Roman troops, he accomplished in three years. Such was the situation at the time of Jesus' birth, history with which Christians are familiar.

When Pilate was sent back to Rome and a new prefect, Marcellus (37-44 A.D.), named, the great persecution of the early Christian church had begun, events associated with Stephen and with Paul, both of whom qualified as Hellenized Jews.

This brief history may suggest to you some of the causes of first century tension, prejudice and hostility between the Jews of Judea and those Jews living among Gentiles in other parts of the Roman Empire.

Consequences Of This History In The Life Of Paul:

1. Most of the Hellenized Jews spoke Greek and studied the Greek Old Testament. The Jews of Jerusalem spoke Aramaic and studied the Hebrew Old Testament.

2. The Jews of Judea valued the first five books of the Bible, called the Torah or the Teachings. Next in value to them were the prophets, of which Elijah was the foremost. Then, all other writings with the Psalter (the psalms) most important for worship.

3. The Jews of the *Diaspora,* on the other hand, valued first the 10 books not included in the Palestinian Old Testament, those which detail the conquests of Alexander through the Western Mediterranean.

4. In the Hellenized world, Jews and Gentiles tolerated each other because Jews conducted much of the commerce of the countries. In Palestine, however, hatred of the Romans was acute because, although the Jews had successfully withstood Alexander, they had been able to keep out the Romans after a century of Jewish independence.

5. In the first century, the Jerusalem Jews considered themselves to be the pure Jews. The Hellenized Jews seemed to agree

they were "number 2;" some tried harder by obeying the strict letter of the law, and to outdo the "pure" Jews in zeal against the early Christian church. As far as Jerusalem Jews were concerned, however, no matter how hard a Hellenized Jew might try, he was contaminated, not one of them.

6. The prejudice against the Greek-speaking Jews is made clear in the New Testment when Stephen and the other six were chosen to look into complaints of the Greek-speaking widows. These widows were being passed over in the distribution of clothes and food, money for which was collected each Friday in the market and placed in a fund called the *Kuppa*, a word meaning basket.

7. Paul's life story is illuminated when this complicated state of affairs in the Mediterranean is realized and understood.

Study Material

Secular history which helps to establish the dates of events in Paul's life:

1. The return of Pontius Pilate, the Prefect of Judea, to Rome, in A.D. 36. The removal of Pilate and the arrival of Marcellus sets the time for the occasion, the trial and death of Stephen, the subsequent persecution of the church and the conversion of Paul.

2. The famine in the reign of the Emperor Claudius is dated A.D. 46-48. The famine affected the eastern Mediterranean for several years and helps to establish the time of Paul's famine visit to Jerusalem.

3. The edict of Claudius expelling the Jews from Rome is dated A.D. 49. This edict caused Aquila and Priscilla to move from Rome to Corinth, not long before Paul's arrival on Mission II.

4. Junius Gallio Annaeus ruled in Achaia, a senatorial province. A provincial governor normally remained in office for one year and was expected to take his post in early summer. Paul was taken before Gallio at the end of Mission II in Corinth. Depending upon whether Gallio was at the beginning or the end of his year of service, the trial could have occurred in the summer of either A.D. 51 or 52. The latter date is preferred because the arrival of the new governor suggests the occasion for Paul's trial.

5. Porcius Festus succeeded Antonius Felix as the prosecutor of Judea, A.D. 60. On the arrival of the new procurator, Paul appealed to Caesar for trial in Rome.

6. During the reign of the emperor Nero, Rome burned, an event dated June 18, A.D. 64. The subsequent persecution of the Christians suggests the probable cause of Paul's second imprisonment and subsequent martyrdom.

Scripture References

Dialogue 1

His place of birth: Acts 21:39; Acts 22:3

Reference to the cloak: 2 Timothy 4:13

His lineage: Romans 11:1, Philippians 3:5

His Roman citizenship: Acts 22:25-29; Acts 23:27

His speaking of Greek: Acts 21:37

His speaking of Aramaic, the Hebrew language: Acts 21:40; Acts 22:2; Acts 26:14

His Hebrew background: Acts 21:39; Acts 22:3; 2 Corinthians 11:22; Philippians 3:5, 6; Acts 23:6; Galatians 1:14; Acts 26:5

A relative in Jerusalem: Acts 23:16

His schooling — Gamaliel: Acts 22:3

The Martyrdom Of Stephen

Stephen, a Hellenist: Acts 6:1-6

Stephen's trial: Acts 6:8-15

The synagogue of freedom: Acts 6:9

Stephen's face shining: Acts 6:15

Stephen's discourse: Acts 7:1-53

The penalty for blasphemy: Deuteronomy 13:6ff

The laying of clothes at the feet of Paul: Acts 7:58

The stoning of Stephen: Acts 7:54-58a

Paul's furious reaction: Acts 8:3

Paul's vote for the death of Christians: Acts 26:10

Paul and the letter of persecution: Acts 9:1-2; Acts 22:5; Acts 26:12

Paul's conversion experience: Acts 9:3-9; Acts 22:6-16; 12-18; Acts 9:10-18

18

Dialogue 2

Paul's movements after his conversion

His reception in Damascus: Acts 9:19-22

His withdrawal to Arabia; his return to Damascus: Galatians 1:17

Plot and his escape from Damascus: Acts 9:23-25; 2 Corinthians 11:32, 33

His return to Jerusalem: Acts 9:26, 27

His two weeks stay with Peter: Galatians 1:18

Plot and escape to Tarsus via Caesarea: Galatians 1:21; Acts 9:29, 30

With Barnabas to Antioch: Acts 11:22-26

Famine visit to Jerusalem: Acts 11:27-30

His return to Antioch with Barnabas and John Mark: Acts 12:24-25

Related References

Suspicion of the Damascus church: Acts 9:19-22

Suspicion of the Jewish church: Acts 9:26

Paul's calling himself an apostle, a slave of Christ: 1 Corinthians 15:9; Galatians 1:10; 1 Corinthians 9:1

The conversion of Cornelius: Acts 10:3-8

Jewish Christians preaching to the Gentiles in Antioch: Acts 11:19-21

Herod Agrippa's persecution: Acts 12:1-11

Herod Agrippa's death: Acts 12:20-25

Dialogue 3

Paul's first missionary journey: Acts 13:1—Acts 14:26

Paul and Barnabas set apart: Acts 13:2, 3

The conversion of Sergius Paulus: Acts 13:6-12

Mark as cousin of Barnabas: Colossians 4:10

Crucifixion meaning "cursed by God": Deuteronomy 21:23

Paul's illness at Perga: Galatians 4:13

Mark's leaving Paul at Perga: Acts 13:13

Mistaken for gods at Lystra: Acts 14:8-18

The stoning at Lystra: Acts 14:19-20

The return to Antioch: Acts 14:26

The enjoinment to love from another in freedom: Galatians 5:13-15

The Council At Jerusalem

The argument over circumcision: Acts 15:1-5

Peter's experience at Joppa: Acts 11:4-18

The confrontation over Titus: Galatians 2:1-10

Peter's eating with Gentiles: Galatians 2:11-14

Paul's refusal to take John Mark on second journey: Acts 15:37-39

Visit of Silas to Antioch: Acts 15:22

Non-scriptural Reference

Paul described as bald, bandy-legged and talkative: *The Acts of Paul and Thecia,* a second century work

Dialogue 4

The second missionary journey: Acts 15:40—Acts 18:22

Timothy circumcized in Lystra: Acts 16:1-3

Timothy as Paul's beloved son: 1 Corinthians 4:17

Timothy's mind like Paul's: Philippians 2:19, 20

Decision to cross into Europe: Acts 16:6-12

Luke with Paul, Troas to Philippi (the first "we" passage): Acts 16:10-17

Timothy escorts Paul to Athens: 1 Thessalonians 3:1, 2

Paul's Athenian speech: Acts 17:22, 31

Cross as "foolishness" to the Greek: 1 Corinthians 1:18-25

Priscilla and Aquila: Acts 18:1, 2

Crispus baptized by Paul: 1 Corinthians 1:14

Paul, trial before Gallio: Acts 18:12-17

Timothy rejoins Paul at Corinth: 1 Thessalonians 3:6

Return to Antioch: Acts 18:18-22

Dialogue 5

Paul's third missionary journey: Acts 18:22-24
Short visit to Jerusalem: Acts 18:22
Three years in Ephesus: Acts 20:31
News of Corinth from Chloe: 1 Corinthians 1:11
Timothy sent to Corinth with a letter: 1 Corinthians 4:17
Paul's second visit to Corinth: 2 Corinthians 12:14; 13:1, 2
Titus sent to Corinth with letter: 2 Corinthians 2:4, 9; 7:6-12

Paul And Women
No make-up or jewelry: 1 Timothy 2:8-15
Wearing of the veil: 1 Corinthians 11:3-16
Keeping silent in church: 1 Corinthians 14:34, 35
Praying in church allowed: 1 Corinthians 11:5
Omission of Mary in post-resurrection appearances: 1 Corinthians 15:3-7
Male and female — one in Christ: Galatians 3:27, 28
In marriage — equal: 1 Corinthians 7:3, 4
Phoebe, Priscilla — as fellow workers: Romans 16:1-3
Junia as apostle: Romans 16:7
Riot in Ephesus: Acts 19:21-41
Meeting with Titus in Philippi: 2 Corinthians 7:6, 13
Paul's third visit to Corinth: Acts 20:2, 3; 1 Corinthians 16:5-7;
    2 Corinthians 1:16
Paul's intention to visit Rome: Romans 15:22-24; Acts 19:21
Collection among the Gentile churches: Romans 15:25, 26
Meeting with Luke in Philippi ("we" passage): Acts 20:1-15;
    Acts 21:1-18
Story of Eutychus: Acts 20:7-12
Meeting at Miletus with Ephesian elders: Acts 20:17-38
Events in Jerusalem and Caesarea: Acts 21:15-40; Acts
    23:23-35; 25:26
Paul — free in Christ: 1 Corinthians 9:1

Dialogue 6

Journey to Rome and Paul's imprisonment: Acts 27:1—28:31

Luke's journeys with Paul ("we" passage): Acts 27:1—28:16

Paul's Visitors In Rome

Tychicus: Colossians 4:7; Ephesians 6:21

Epaphroditus: Philippians 2:25; 4:18

Timothy: Philippians 1:1; Colossians 1:1; Philemon 1

Onesimus: Philemon

John Mark: Colossians 4:10; 2 Timothy 4:11

Paul's desire to visit Spain: Romans 15:24, 28

Priscilla and Aquila return to Ephesus: 2 Timothy 4:19

The desertion of Demas: 2 Timothy 4:10

Non-scriptural References:

Paul's second arrest in Rome: Eusebius, *Ecclesiastical History* 2.22,2

Paul's death compared to John the Baptist's: Tertullian, *De praescript,* 36

Discussion Questions

All Dialogues

1. What characteristics of Paul are made clear?

2. What method of communicating the Gospel is shown and how successful is it for Paul?

3. From what is Paul set free?

Dialogue 1

1. How did Paul's background prepare him for his ministry to the Gentiles?

2. What in his background had to be overcome?

3. Apply the first two questions to your own Christian life and witness.

4. We often think of prejudice as a modern phenomenon. What prejudices are evident among the Jews of Jerusalem? What positive steps can be taken to overcome prejudice — then and now?

5. What does the route Paul chose to Damascus from Jerusalem have to do with his conversion? How do our ordinary decisions affect our Christian lives?

6. In his conversion experience, what Paul described as light we might understand as inner vision or bright and sudden insight. What effect did the experience have upon Paul? Can you give an example of such sudden change in a person today?

Dialogue 2

1. What kind of story might Paul's soldier-escorts have told to the Sanhedrin? How much effect would that report have had on subsequent relationships between the Jews and Paul? Between Jews and Christians? What responsibility is ours in reporting events?

2. Paul was not received warmly at Damascas. Have you ever seen Christians today give a new convert the cold shoulder? Why?

3. Discuss the characteristics of Ananias and Barnabas. Of what value are such second bananas in the church today?

4. Does the description of Antioch, as well as that of ancient Tarsus, change some of your ideas about life in the world of the first century? What is peculiar about every generation concerning modernity?

5. How did the death of Herod Agrippa change the climate for the early Christians? In what ways do today's rulers affect the lives of Christians? Give some examples.

Dialogue 3

1. What circumstances allowed Paul and Barnabas to start their first missionary journey? What circumstances must occur in the church today for such possibilities to appear?

2. For Paul and Barnabas to go to Cyprus seemed natural. How could our churches make such Christian service natural today?

3. What possibly made Mark turn back at Perga? Under what circumstances have you seen such Christian behavior today?

4. What were Paul's justifications for his anger with John Mark? When and why have you felt such disgust and anger with a fellow Christian?

5. From the beginnings of the early church, many nationalities were numbered among the believers; in your area, what are church patterns today?

6. Our feelings about the cross make it difficult for us to appreciate the Jews' troubled thoughts. But what if the death of Jesus had taken place in our time, and he had been put to death in the electric chair?

7. What made the decision at the council of Jerusalem of extreme importance to the early church? And to us?

Dialogue 4

1. Paul and Barnabas fought over John Mark's going on the second missionary journey. What have you seen Christians today fighting over? Comment on the results, then and now, of such in-fighting.

2. What did Paul's going into Macedonia mean to the early church? What has it meant to you and to the church through the years?

3. Paul seems to have been frustrated in Athens. Articulate the conflict between Greek and Hebrew thought. How does that same conflict exist today in your training and Christian life? In what ways does it affect you? Why would Paul (or you) rather have opposition than amused disdain?

4. Compare or contrast the spread of the Gospel to Rome with the spread of the Gospel in your denomination today.

5. How do you account for the rapid growth of Christianity among such rotten people as the Corinthians? Today, the church still works with such disadvantaged people; what difference do you see in our approach? In the results?

Dialogue 5

1. Paul is often charged with responsibility for holding back women in the church. How does he justify his stand? What else could he have done? How do you account for the different status of women in the western church from that of the eastern and southern churches today?

2. Consider another accusation against Paul — that he was concerned only with evangelism, not with social problems. What in his ministry refutes this charge? In what ways has the balance between the two concerns shifted today?

3. How did the politics in Rome and Judea affect Paul when he returned to Jerusalem? What Christians in the world today are affected by politics of their own and other countries?

4. What irony happened when Festus and Agrippa refused to free Paul? In what misfortune for a Christian have you seen a similar ironic occurrence?

Dialogue 6

1. Consider the reactions of the sailors, the prisoners and Paul's to the terrible storm on the trip to Rome. How do you, as a Christian individual, react when things go wrong?

2. Think back over Paul's early Christian life, especially his harsh treatment of John Mark, his quarrels with Barnabas, his attack on Peter's eating with Gentiles until the Jews came to Antioch. Then consider his behavior on shipboard, the love shown to him by the elders at Miletus, his struggles and reconciliation with the Corinthians, his evident reconciliation with John Mark, Luke's staying with him to the end. What has happened to Paul? The specifics may differ, but what occurs in the constant, faithful Christian life no matter what century it is lived in? How can understanding Paul's life affect your own?

3. Consider Paul's deep desire to go to Rome and to Spain; what is being suggested about strategy in the Christian church? Is that strategy still valid in the world today? Why or why not?

4. Think about Paul's last days in prison. How have you coped with disappointment in, desertion of, and betrayal by friends?

Dialogue 1
Paul's Early Life Through His Conversion

Woman: Paul! Paul! May I speak with you?

Paul: Of course, of course. *(pause)* Do I know you?

Woman: No, no. I'm a traveler, Paul —

Paul: So am I!

Woman: I've traveled all through Southern Europe and the Eastern Mediterranean —

Paul: So have I!

Woman: I've become interested in your life.

Paul: *(surprised)* In my life? Why is that?

Woman: Everywhere I went I heard your name. And I've read some of your letters —

Paul: *(pleased)* Some of my letters have survived then? Good, good. I'm glad of that. Well then, where shall we begin?

Woman: Let's begin at the beginning. Where were you born?

Paul: Tarsus! No mean city that — a Greek city, capital of the Roman district of Cilicia — in Asia Minor.

Woman: Uh, Paul — we call Asia Minor — uh, Turkey now.

Paul: Turkey? *(laughing)* That's funny. You've traveled there, have you?

Woman: Oh yes . . .

Paul: *(eagerly)* Have you seen Tarsus?

Woman: *(hesitates)* No. Uh, Paul your — your Tarsus — has disappeared.

30

Paul: *(stunned)* Not my beautiful city — not the marble temples, the pillars —

Woman: I'm sorry, Paul.

Paul: *(incredulous)* The libraries?

Woman: Everything, Paul. Everything.

Paul: *(fiercely)* Don't tell me that! Nothing could destroy the towering peaks of the Taurus mountains, the firs, the pines, the dark valleys full of rushing water — I saw those things every morning of my boyhood.

Woman: You're right, Paul. They are still there — and the enormous herds of black goats wandering across the plains — they are still there.

Paul: Ah yes, the goats! Do they still make that tough cloth from the goat's hair?

Woman: Yes — for tents and sails and rope —

Paul: *(eagerly)* And the cloaks? Do they still make the cloaks?

Woman: I saw the goat herders wearing square-shouldered cloaks —

Paul: The very ones! Many's the time I've seen a man step out of his cloak and set it stiff and upright on the ground. Wonderful cloaks to keep out the cold. I begged Timothy to bring me one.

Woman: *(surprised)* When?

Paul: At the last — when I was in the prison at Rome.

Woman: You knew about the goat's cloth when you were a boy, Paul?

Paul: I should tell you — as a boy I was called Saul, not Paul. My father named me for the first king of Israel. But yes, I knew a lot about that cloth — learned to make tents with it.

31

Woman: Forgive me, Paul — but your voice, your manner — they don't seem to be the voice and manner of a laborer.

Paul: *(laughing)* You know little about Jews! Every Jewish father saw to it that his son was taught a useful trade — mine was making tents.

Woman: Your father — who was he?

Paul: *(with pride)* A man of the tribe of Benjamin, a Pharisee, one of a small colony of Jews in the Greek city of Tarsus.

Woman: So — you were brought up as a Jew in a Greek city —

Paul: *(laughing)* And as a Roman citizen!

Woman: *(bewildered)* How did you become a Roman citizen?

Paul: I didn't "become" a Roman citizen — I was born one! Tarsus was a "free" city from the days of Mark Antony. You know Mark Antony?

Woman: Only from Shakespeare — uh, that's an English writer — I always think of Mark Antony and Cleopatra.

Paul: So do I. It was Tarsus to which Mark Antony welcomed Cleopatra! I heard that story many times. And it was Mark Antony who gave Roman citizenship to all men of high standing in Tarsus — rights that were later confirmed by Augustus Caesar.

Woman: Then Tarsus, though it was Greek, was governed by the Romans?

Paul: In the final analysis, yes. Locally, however, it was governed by Greek philosophers.

Woman: A city — governed by philosophers?

Paul: Yes. Plato's idea. You've heard of him?

Woman: Uh huh.

Paul: Tarsus was governed mostly by Stoics and Epicureans from the University of Tarsus.

Woman: *(in astonishment)* Tarsus had a University?

Paul: *(tartly)* Why yes, of course! A fine one. Our schools surpassed even those of Athens and Alexandria.

Woman: You spoke Greek, I suppose.

Paul: Of course *(quickly and vehemently)* I spoke Aramaic too — the language of the Hebrews. I was a Jew of the Jews, a Hebrew of the Hebrews, a Pharisee of the Pharisees!

Woman: And the Gentiles of Tarsus — did they accept Jews?

Paul: *(his good humor restored)* They had to put up with us!

Woman: Why?

Paul: Because Jews controlled the commerce of the city.

Woman: A little resentment then — perhaps?

Paul: Yes. Partly because we had the money — partly because Jews were exempt from military service — but —

Woman: Some deeper cause?

Paul: Well, look at it from the Gentile point of view. To them, we must have been a curious lot — not eating pork or shellfish — ignoring their games and their marble gods, disappearing into our mysterious, dark synagogues every Sabbath!

Woman: Still, you did have a strong Hellenistic background.

Paul: Perhaps so. But my father saw to it that I was no Hellenist. I received detailed instruction in Jewish law.

Woman: From a rabbi?

Paul: In Tarsus, yes. And then my father sent me to Jerusalem to study.

Woman: Oh? When?

Paul: When I was about 13 or so.

33

Woman: That's pretty young to go away from home.

Paul: I had relatives in Jerusalem, and besides —

Woman: You wanted to go?

Paul: It was the dream of every Jewish boy in the Roman empire to return to the city of his forefathers — to the holy city — Jerusalem!

Woman: The idea of travel didn't frighten you?

Paul: Why — travel hung in the very air of Tarsus. Before I was born, our men had cut through the Sicilian Gates!

Woman: *(delighted)* I saw that mountain pass! A marvelous feat of engineering — it opened the way to Ephesus —

Paul: And beyond that — to Rome. Even as a boy, I dreamed of going some day to Rome!

Woman: But for now — reared among the sights and sounds of departure and return, a young Jewish boy —

Paul: Started happily off for Jerusalem!

Woman: And did that boy enjoy his boat trip?

Paul: *(dreamily)* Oh yes. I can recall it now — the smell of the sheep tied to the rail, the chill of the wind, the hiss of water running along the side of the ship, the riding lights bobbing against the sky —

Woman: You didn't sleep much!

Paul: *(laughing)* Who could sleep!

Woman: Where did you leave ship?

Paul: At Caesarea —

Woman: Then, then Jerusalem lay south.

Paul: *(agreeing)* Hmm. *(eagerly)* I could hardly wait to see it! We passed camels padding softly in the dust, girls drawing water at the wells, scattered brown villages clinging to the slopes of the hills. With each turn of the mountain road, my heart beat faster. Finally — *(sighs)*

Woman: What did you see first?

Paul: *(exultantly)* The gold-brown stones of Herod's tower —

Woman: *(indulgently)* You sound as if your feet scarcely touched the ground.

Paul: *(laughing)* They didn't! But Gamaliel brought me back to earth in a hurry!

Woman: Gamaliel?

Paul: My teacher, a Pharisee and a member of the Sanhedrin — a great teacher.

Woman: Exactly what did he teach you?

Paul: Everything! Everything I wanted to become a member of the Sanhedrin too. But especially the Jewish law. I loved the intricacies of the law, that law hammered into the very stones of Jerusalem.

Woman: *(chattily)* When I traveled in Jerusalem, our guide pointed out the stone cliff where Stephen had died.

Paul: *(shrinking back)* They do that?

Woman: *(dismayed)* Yes. I'm sorry, Paul.

Paul: It haunts me. *(shaking his head)* Even today, it haunts me.

Woman: Does your love of the law explain your part in Stephen's death?

Paul: *(slowly)* If it can be explained.

Woman: Exactly who was Stephen?

Paul: One of the seven chosen by the Christian Jews to look into the complaints of Greek-speaking widows.

Woman: Complaints? What complaints?

Paul: They weren't being included in the distribution —

Woman: *(bewildered)* Of what?

Paul: *(impatiently)* You really don't know anything about Jews, do you? Every Friday morning, money was collected from people in the market and put in a fund called the *Kuppa*, a word that means "basket." Then, each day, those in need, usually widows, received money or food or clothing —

Woman: And these Greek-speaking widows, though they were Jews, were being passed over?

Paul: *(nodding)* Deliberately so.

Woman: *(not understanding)* Why?

Paul: Prejudice. *(pause, politely)* Perhaps you have none in your country?

Woman: *(lamely)* Uh, some, yes. And this prejudice of yours?

Paul: It goes back a long way. Judea had suffered persecution —

Woman: *(brightly)* From the Romans, you mean?

Paul: *(losing patience)* No, no, no! About 400 years before that! Persecution from the Syrians, under Antiochus —

Woman: He scattered the Jews?

Paul: Yes. By my day, most of the Jewish nation lived outside of Palestine. *(a rush of feeling)* And yet, Palestinian Jews looked down on us — the Jews of the *diaspora!*

Woman: But why? They were all Jews, weren't they? Why?

Paul: *(deliberately as to a backward child)* Because the scattered Jews spoke Greek and lived in the defiling presence of the Gentiles. The Palestinians called us Hellenists!

Woman: So you and Stephen were both Hellenists.

Paul: *(vehemently)* Not at all! Not at all! I was a Jew of the Jews, a Hebrew —

Woman: *(hastily interrupting)* I gather Stephen did far more than care for widows?

Paul: Yes. He went about preaching. We brought Stephen to trial when he attacked the two things most precious to the Jews — the Temple and the Law.

Woman: The Sanhedrin wouldn't like that. Where was the trial?

Paul: In the synagogue of the Freedmen.

Woman: Freedmen? Who are the Freedmen?

Paul: Descendants of those Jews persecuted under Alexander.

Woman: *(timidly)* Uh, not the same persecution as the Syrian one?

Paul: *(impatiently)* No, no, of course not. Why, we had enjoyed 100 years of independence, won for us by guerilla forces under Judas Maccabeus — glorious days for Jews — *(bitterly)* brought to an end by the Romans in 63 B.C. That's when Pompey marched into Palestine and conquered Jerusalem.

Woman: *(getting him back on the track)* But the Freedmen? Who were they?

Paul: Jews marched off as slaves to Rome by Pompey — but later freed.

Woman: Oh, I see — the synagogue honors them. What was the trial like?

Paul: Similar to the one held for Jesus — the form never changed. The members of the Sanhedrin, the judges, sat in a semi-circle with the High Priest in the center.

Woman: Was testimony written down?

Paul: Of course! It was a court of law! A secretary, one at each end of the semi-circle, took notes, one for the prosecution, one for the defense. And then, of course, there were the law students.

Woman: The law students? What were they doing at the trial?

Paul: Where else were they to learn? They sat on three benches in front of the judges.

Woman: And Stephen? Where did he sit?

Paul: He was supposed to stand before the judges in an attitude of humiliation.

Woman: But he didn't?

Paul: Stephen stood there, his head up, his face shining.

Woman: How did Stephen answer the charges?

Paul: *(shaking his head)* He never did. He recited the history of Israel from Abraham to Solomon —

Woman: *(dryly)* Familiar ground to the Sanhedrin, I should think.

Paul: *(shaking his head)* Not the way Stephen recast it! He told our history in terms of Jewish opposition to God's appointed guides.

Woman: Could the court deny his charge?

Paul: No. But Stephen brought that history up to date, calling us, among other things, "stiff-necked," "unconverted in heart," "opposers of God's Holy Spirit."

Woman: I bet those words caused a few gasps!

Paul: If only he had stopped there! But, imagine if you can — Stephen, standing in a Jewish temple, where Jews believe that there, and only there, can men know God — Stephen, thundering "the most High dwells not in temples made with hands!"

38

Woman: I can imagine —

Paul: *(going right on)* Stephen, standing before men who believed with all their hearts that the law given to Moses was complete and forever perfect — Stephen, declaring that the law of Moses had been replaced by the law of Christ! We were stunned!

Woman: Did Stephen seem frightened?

Paul: Not at all. Into the quiet he dropped these words, "Behold, I see the heavens opened, and the Son of Man standing on the right hand of God!"

Woman: For a Jew, wouldn't that be blasphemy?

Paul: *(nodding)* Indeed so. And the penalty for blasphemy is death. We rushed at him — and grabbed him!

Woman: It sounds like a lynching —

Paul: *(remembering)* Caught up in a blind uncontrollable anger, we dragged him out of Jerusalem through the Damascus gate. On the way, the men picked up stones —

Woman: You too, Paul?

Paul: No. At the edge of a cliff, they laid their clothes at my feet. As I watched, they threw Stephen over that cliff. Stephen staggered to his feet. Then I saw him kneel — and I heard him pray, "Lord Jesus, receive my spirit."

Woman: He prayed? With stones falling on him?

Paul: *(nodding)* With stones raining on him. And Stephen called out loud and clear, "Lord, lay this not to their charge."

Woman: Like the cry of Jesus on the cross!

Paul: *(intensely)* As I watched Stephen die, forgiving us — I went crazy. That day, that very day, I dragged Christians into the street, put some in prison and had some killed. *(muttering)* Madness. Madness.

Woman: *(anxiously)* Paul, are you all right?

Paul: Yes, yes, of course. I'm sorry — but sometimes — when I remember —

Woman: It's understandable, Paul. Perhaps if we went back a little?

Paul: Of course, of course.

Woman: I remember that in the trials of Jesus — well, I thought only the Roman government, not the Sanhedrin, could pronounce the death sentence.

Paul: *(nodding)* That's true.

Woman: Then why did the Romans let you get away with it?

Paul: Ah — a good question. Do you remember Pontius Pilate?

Woman: Who could forget him?

Paul: Well, after the crucifixion of Jesus, discipline completely broke down in Jerusalem. Pilate was called back to Rome to answer to the Emperor —

Woman: But I don't see —

Paul: *(interrupting)* At the time of Stephen's trial, the new prefect, Marcellus, had just arrived in Jerusalem. He didn't care to tangle with the Sanhedrin. And, frankly, he didn't care what Jews did to Christians.

Woman: I see. Paul, after the fury of the moment died down, did the persecution of the Christian Jews stop?

Paul: Quite the contrary. I myself voted to put Christians to death.

Woman: Paul — *(shocked)* How can you justify that?

Paul: I can't. Not now. But at that time I was afraid the Jerusalem Jews might think I was partial to the Greek-speaking Jews —

Woman: Because you too had come from outside of Jerusalem?

Paul: Yes. But also, I sensed a turning point had been reached.

Woman: In what way?

Paul: Up until Stephen's trial, Jews who believed in Christ differed in no discernible fashion from those who did not believe.

Woman: You mean both orthodox Jews and Christian Jews went to the synagogues?

Paul: Yes. And both kept the Jewish law.

Woman: *(comprehending)* Ah — and then Stephen —

Paul: Stephen challenged those practices for Christian Jews.

Woman: *(protesting)* But Stephen stood trial and lost!

Paul: *(slowly)* Did he?

Woman: *(comprehending)* You couldn't forget him, could you?

Paul: No, I couldn't. In my mind, I saw his face, I heard his words. I had to ask myself what secret took Stephen to his death with such serenity.

Woman: And that preoccupation plunged you into even more violent action?

Paul: Reaction, it was. When the news came that Christians were active in Damascus, I had to go; I had to.

Woman: What possible right could you have to interfere in another city?

Paul: The Jews in Damascus were, theoretically, under the authority of the high priest in Jerusalem.

Woman: Oh, I see. So, the high priest of Jerusalem could send you there.

Paul: Not without permission from the Romans. Marcellus gave Joseph Caiaphas a letter, granting power to pursue fugitives from Jerusalem.

Woman: And Joseph Caiaphas gave this letter to you?

Paul: I asked for it. I had to prove to the Palestinian Jews I was a real Jew. I had to go to Damascus.

Woman: Let's see now. If I remember rightly, it's about 140 miles from Jerusalem to Damascus.

Paul: About that far. I had the choice of two roads — the shorter one down to Jericho, going north along the Jordan valley —

Woman: Did you go that way?

Paul: No. Too hot that time of year. I chose the other way. *(pause)* Or perhaps it was chosen for me.

Woman: You went then, the longer way — through Samaria and Galilee into the Lebanon mountains. You went on foot?

Paul: By donkey —

Woman: A long journey in any case.

Paul: About two weeks.

Woman: Did you go alone?

Paul: I had an escort of Sanhedrin police. But, since I was a Pharisee, I had nothing to do with them.

Woman: A lonely trip, then —

Paul: Nothing to do but — think.

Woman: And watch the passing scene.

Paul: Which only gave me more to think about. Everywhere, I saw reminders of Jesus. The Sea of Galilee and the villages exactly as they were when he was alive. Capernaum, and, fronting the lake, the synagogue where he had preached. *(slowly)* And I walked the very roads where he had walked.

Woman: And saw the men and women —

Paul: Who had seen and followed him.

Woman: You must have been in a turmoil.

Paul: My heart boiled — *(slowly)* — with what I thought was hate.

Woman: Let me see now — that road starts to rise, uh —

Paul: Just past the Sea of Galilee. We climbed into the Lebanon mountains, through hills, browned by the sun and dotted with stones. Near the top, the Jordan forks and slides down the hill to Galilee. It was noon — behind me lay Jerusalem — in front of me Damascus.

Woman: You must have been hot — at noon —

Paul: Yes. But the wind blew cold up there as the daily storm clouds gathered.

Woman: Daily storm clouds?

Paul: Almost every day, about noon, the hot air from the plains meets the cold air of the mountain range —

Woman: Oh, of course. I remember. I was in a storm up there — violent electrical storm.

Paul: *(rising emotion)* It was then I saw the light —

Woman: You mean the lightning?

Paul: No! Not lightning! A light — an unbearable light! A light brighter than the sun. I put my hands over my eyes and fell to the ground. And then —

Woman: What Paul?

Paul: The sound of a voice.

Woman: Did the police hear the voice?

Paul: Some saw only the light. Others heard only the voice.

Woman: What did the voice say?

Paul: The voice called me by name — by my childhood name. "Saul, Saul, why do you persecute me?" I stammered, "Who are you, Lord?"

43

Woman: And the answer?

Paul: "I am Jesus, whom you are persecuting."

Woman: And so you were suddenly converted — ?

Paul: I suddenly surrendered. But *(with conviction)* my conversion must have begun with Stephen.

Woman: Paul — how do you explain what happened — the light and the voice?

Paul: *(with spirit)* I don't need any explanation!

Woman: For us in the 20th century then?

Paul: For you, then, I might say that, in some way, the limitations of my physical body had been shattered.

Woman: Just for a few moments — ?

Paul: Long enough for me to perceive the reality of the risen Christ — long enough to accept his discipleship for my life; long enough *(pause)* long enough to suffer the humiliation of such love. A love that, in spite of my murderous heart, had set me free — free from my sinful self!

Woman: Thank you, Paul. We will talk again.

Dialogue 2
The Years Of Suspicion

Woman: Paul, when we left off talking the last time, you were lying on the Damascus road. What happened?

Paul: The voice told me to go into the city. But when I opened my eyes, I, who had perceived reality, could not see the Damascus road.

Woman: You were blind?

Paul: Yes, blind. *(short laugh)* I, who had planned to sweep through that city like an avenging fury, was led into Damascus, helpless as a child.

Woman: Where did the Sanhedrin police take you?

Paul: Through the East Gate of Damascus to a street called "Straight."

Woman: *(excitedly)* I know that street. It runs straight as an arrow from the east to the west — through Damascus. It's an odd street, space in the center for auto traffic, and then on each side people walk among the merchants who sit under awnings.

Paul: *(nodding)* The same as in my day, except the "traffic" was chariots then. Well — because I had previously planned to stay at the house of a Jew named Judas, I had the police take me there. And they, no doubt glad to be rid of me, went back to Jerusalem.

Woman: With a strange story, indeed, to tell.

Paul: *(wryly)* One I'm sure they lost no time in telling to the Sanhedrin!

Woman: I don't know how you managed — all alone and blind. Did your landlord take care of you?

Paul: No! He wanted no part of me. For three days I neither ate nor drank. It was as though my body had been shattered, in some curious way verifying the truth of what had happened to me.

Woman: Alone — blind — no food or drink — who rescued you?

Paul: Ananias, a Jewish Christian — *(slowly)* — one who had fled from Jerusalem to get away from me.

Woman: How could he possibly have been persuaded to help you?

Paul: In a dream God told him to come to me.

Woman: But still, Ananias knew what you were —

Paul: *(sharply)* Correction, please. He knew what I had been.

Woman: Sorry, Paul. Still, he must have been afraid.

Paul: I'm sure he was. But, afraid or not, his first words to me were "Brother Saul."

Woman: "Brother Saul!" Strange words from a man you had meant to kill!

Paul: Strange indeed. And Ananias laid his hands on me — *(slowly)* — it was as if scales fell from my eyes —

Woman: You could see again?

Paul: Yes. Then Ananias dipped his hand into a basin of water and baptized me. And he told me — he told me —

Woman: What, Paul?

Paul: That I would bring Christ's name, not only to the Jews, but to kings and Gentiles.

Woman: Did you understand?

46

Paul: I couldn't comprehend that — not then. Ananias gave me food and water. When I felt stronger, he took me to his house to meet the Damascus followers of Jesus.

Woman: *(dryly)* That must have been a very interesting meeting!

Paul: *(laughing shortly)* They didn't know what to make of me.

Woman: Nor what to do with you!

Paul: They didn't trust me.

Woman: Well, you could hardly blame them, Paul!

Paul: *(stubbornly)* Just the same — because I was a changed man — I went right into the synagogue to preach. I was determined everyone should know it.

Woman: Forgive me, Paul. But that was foolish.

Paul: You're right. It was foolish; I finally realized that. I needed some time to be alone, to think through what had happened to me.

Woman: There weren't too many places you could go.

Paul: You're right. *(dryly)* I wasn't exactly welcome in Damascus. And I couldn't go back to Jerusalem! So — I went south — to Arabia.

Woman: Let's see — Mount Sinai lies there — by the Red Sea.

Paul: Yes, the mountain where Moses had received the Law. *(slowly)* The very source of the Law I had loved all my life —

Woman: Did you stay in Arabia long?

Paul: Long enough to face steadfastly what my lot would be. To the followers of the Messiah, I would be suspect.

Woman: They could think you were a kind of secret agent, out to destroy them from within.

Paul: Exactly. And as I had hunted down the Christians, so would the Jews hunt me down.

Woman: Perhaps with even more zeal?

Paul: Yes, because I had been a member of the Sanhedrin.

Woman: After Arabia, where did you go?

Paul: Back to Damascus.

Woman: You preached?

Paul: And taught —

Woman: With success?

Paul: Not much. Only a few converts in three years. And then Roman soldiers came to arrest me.

Woman: Why — why after so long a time?

Paul: Aretas, the governor of Judea sent them. He was having difficulties with Herod Agrippa. Aretas knew that if he could capture or kill me, he would gain favor with the Jews. And with Herod. But one of my friends heard a soldier mention my name. And he saw the guards waiting at the city gates.

Woman: Why, walls go all around the city — walls wide enough to drive on!

Paul: Yes. But the upper story of my house rose above the rampart; through the window I could look out to the open desert.

Woman: Oh, I see.

Paul: That night friends lowered me in a basket to the wall.

Woman: And you were able to drop over the face of the wall?

Paul: *(bitterly)* Only to go creeping from shadow to shadow in the night.

Woman: Paul, you don't sound too happy about that escape!

Paul: There's something ridiculous, even humiliating, about a grown man being lowered in a basket — it still rankles. *(outburst)* Am I not an Apostle?

Woman: *(bewildered)* Yes.

Paul: *(forcefully)* Was I not a slave of Christ?

Woman: Yes —

Paul: *(with force)* Then why was I running away?

Woman: *(laughing)* Oh Paul! No one would call escape from murderers running away! Where did you go?

Paul: *(vigorously)* To Jerusalem!

Woman: *(astonished)* To the lair of the enemy? *(outburst)* Paul, you're a fool!

Paul: Perhaps. But if so, a fool for Christ.

Woman: You slipped into a quiet place, I hope.

Paul: Not exactly. I went to the synagogue where we had tried Stephen.

Woman: Weren't you afraid?

Paul: *(forcefully)* No, I wasn't afraid. But the Christians were!

Woman: Of you?

Paul: Of course! Of course. They were suspicious of me.

Woman: All the Christians? The leaders?

Paul: Especially the leaders! *(pause)* All except one — Barnabas.

Woman: Who's Barnabas?

Paul: A Christian Jew, a native of Cyprus, a man who had known me in Damascus.

Woman: He helped you?

Paul: He took me to the apostles.

Woman: To Peter, you mean?

Paul: And to James, the brother of Jesus. And all the others in the Jerusalem council.

Woman: Barnabas vouched for you?

Paul: He surely did. He told of my work during the three years in Damascus.

Woman: And the council accepted you?

Paul: Reluctantly — and then only on the word of Barnabas.

Woman: *(admiringly)* A well thought of man!

Paul: Indeed he was — a remarkable man. When everyone else believed the worst of me, Barnabas believed the best. When everyone else called me a fake, he insisted I was a genuine believer.

Woman: Then Barnabas didn't hold your past against you?

Paul: Not at all. Not at all.

Woman: Paul, it seems we owe you to the Christians you met — to the forgiving prayer of Stephen, to the brotherly spirit of Ananias and to the large-hearted nature of Barnabas.

Paul: To that list add Cephas.

Woman: Peter?

Paul: Yes. I stayed with him for two weeks in Jerusalem. He taught me about Jesus.

Woman: You mean he filled in the gaps of your knowledge?

Paul: Yes — of Christ's earthly life. No one could teach me of his resurrected life. I had experienced the risen Lord. And that's what I preached.

Woman: You preached in Jerusalem?

Paul: Yes. But —

Woman: Let me guess — trouble started.

Paul: Among the Greek-speaking Jews. They remembered Stephen.

Woman: Big trouble?

Paul: They tried to murder me.

Woman: And the Jewish Christians?

Paul: I think, in the plot, they saw a reason to get rid of me. They hustled me up to the harbor at Caesarea and packed me off —

Woman: Where?

Paul: To Tarsus.

Woman: I imagine when you had gone, both the Jews and the Christians of Jerusalem heaved sighs of relief!

Paul: Yes. But not I.

Woman: How many years were you in Tarsus?

Paul: Four long years. For the sake of my Jewish father, I was — tolerated.

Woman: The hometown boy sent back in disgrace?

Paul: Exactly. But I put my stay to good use, studying, preaching and teaching. But I marked time there in Tarsus, fearing, indeed knowing, that the churches in Judea had gladly forgotten me!

Woman: Who or what brought this fallow period of your life to an end?

Paul: The "who" was Barnabas.

Woman: Barnabas again! And the "what?"

Paul: Antioch.

Woman: Oh yes — in Syria — about 300 miles north of Jerusalem. What was happening in Antioch?

Paul: You see — after the death of Stephen and during the persecution —

Woman: The persecution you had a hand in?

Paul: *(wearily)* You see how people never forget? Yes, yes — the one I had a hand in. The followers of Jesus were scattered as far away as the island of Cyprus.

Woman: Where they preached and taught?

Paul: Yes, but only to Jews. And then some of the Christian Jews from Cyprus — and from Cyrene — came to Antioch and taught, not only to Jews — but to Gentiles!

Woman: That had never happened before?

Paul: Not deliberately. But there was a Gentile convert named Cornelius.

Woman: Cornelius?

Paul: A centurion from Caesarea. Peter baptized him. But it was not Peter who looked for Cornelius — it was Cornelius who sought out Peter.

Woman: But why would he do that?

Paul: *(patiently)* He was a God-fearer.

Woman: *(exasperated)* Paul — you keep springing things on me I never heard of! What's a God-fearer?

Paul: A non-Jew who had adopted the Jewish code of morality.

Woman: Not a full convert to Judaism, then?

Paul: No, not a Jew at all. A God-fearer attended services — in the court of the Gentiles — but he made no sacrifices. Nor was he circumcized.

Woman: Were there many God-fearers?

Paul: Oh yes. Especially in Antioch. And when the Jewish Christians told their story in the synagogue, many Gentiles, like Cornelius, responded.

Woman: And the church in Jerusalem got a little worried!

Paul: They did indeed. They sent Barnabas to Antioch to look into things.

Woman: And when he saw the Gentiles becoming believers — ?

Paul: He hunted for me. And when he found me in Tarsus, I was more than delighted to go to Antioch.

Woman: Was Antioch a good city?

Paul: It depends on what you mean by good. It was the third largest city in the world, the seat of the Roman governor. It had a fine climate. And it certainly was modern.

Woman: *(laughing, disbelieving)* Modern? In what ways?

Paul: The houses had central heating, lights — plumbing —

Woman: Plumbing!

Paul: Why yes. Fresh water from the Orantes River was directed through every house.

Woman: Well! I had no idea. But, in other ways, was it a good city?

Paul: As far as morality goes, no. Have you ever heard of the Groves of Daphne?

Woman: Some kind of pleasure garden?

Paul: A huge garden dedicated to the worship of the river god — a scene of incredible orgiastic rituals — revolting to all men and women of decency!

Woman: Did that revulsion account for the great number of God-fearers in Antioch?

Paul: Yes — yes indeed.

Woman: When was it, Paul, that you went to Antioch?

Paul: About the year 47.

53

Woman: Astonishing! *(excitedly)* Paul, while you were working in Antioch — Claudius marched out of Rome and into Britain!

Paul: *(calmly)* Oh yes, I know — a country of barbarians —

Woman: Paul!

Paul: I heard many a story about the soldiers pegging out their tents beside the river Thames.

Woman: *(slowly)* On a hill, Paul — on a hill that someday would hold a great cathedral bearing your name.

Paul: How little we know! How little we know. I'm glad that Britain became Christian.

Woman: So am I! Paul, I notice that sometimes you call the believers the followers of Jesus or of the Messiah, sometimes you say Jewish Christians, sometimes you simply say Christians.

Paul: It was in Antioch that we were first called Christians. We didn't call ourselves that — not at first.

Woman: Oh? Then how did you get the name?

Paul: The people of Antioch were famous for handing out nicknames. When the emperor Julian, who had a beard, came to visit Antioch, they called him The Goat.

Woman: Oh! The word Christian then was not intended as a compliment?

Paul: No indeed. The Greek word for Messiah is *Christos.* The ending "ian" means followers of. They spit out Christian at us in contempt!

Woman: But if the people of Antioch took the trouble to nickname the followers of Jesus, the church must have been growing — visibly.

Paul: Hundreds became Christians, both Jews and Gentiles.

Woman: More than at Jerusalem, the mother church?

Paul: Many more. But the bond between the churches held firm. Why, when the famine came —

Woman: Famine?

Paul: About a year or so after I had gone to Antioch — Claudius was still reigning in Rome — famine struck Judea — hardest of all in Jerusalem.

Woman: And the church at Antioch?

Paul: Collected money and sent it with Barnabas and me to Jerusalem!

Woman: Your first visit since the time you came uninvited from Damascus!

Paul: *(laughing)* With quite a different reception! I was welcomed with open arms! But the Jerusalem church was suffering, not only from famine, but from a new persecution.

Woman: The Sanhedrin again?

Paul: Not this time. Herod Agrippa was behind this persecution.

Woman: You mentioned him before, I believe, in connection with the Damascus plot. You know, Paul, there are entirely too many Herods!

Paul: And with good reason! Herod the great, the one in power when Jesus was born, married 10 times!

Woman: And was Herod Agrippa that Herod's son?

Paul: No, no — his grandson. Herod Agrippa's father was Aristobulus — drowned by his own father.

Woman: *(shuddering)* Ugh. And his mother?

Paul: Mariamne, a direct descendant of the Maccabees.

Woman: And Herod Agrippa, her son, cultivated his Jewish heritage?

Paul: Like his grandfather — when it suited him. Publicly, he kept the law —

Woman: To get in good with the Jews?

Paul: Exactly so. And for the same reason, he killed James.

Woman: Which James?

Paul: One of the 12, the brother of John. And when he saw how popular that murder made him, he arrested Peter.

Woman: *(bewildered)* Why didn't he kill Peter too?

Paul: Because he couldn't during the days of unleavened bread.

Woman: *(exasperated)* I'm sorry, but what has that to do with anything?

Paul: *(sighing)* Oh, you Gentiles! *(patiently)* On Passover, and for the seven days following — by Jewish law — no execution could be carried out.

Woman: Oh, I see. When Peter was taken, the Chrisians must have been terrified.

Paul: They gathered at Mary's house, the mother of John Mark —

Woman: John Mark?

Paul: A cousin of Barnabas. The Christians met at Mary's house to pray for Peter. But they had little hope — he was guarded by four squads of soldiers, one squad for each watch.

Woman: How many in a squad?

Paul: Four. They chained Peter between two soldiers — two others watched the door.

Woman: What happened?

Paul: Peter did escape, but only he could tell you how. But the hand of God was surely in it.

Woman: Quite a set-back for Herod Agrippa!

Paul: He flew into a rage and had all 16 guards killed.

Woman: And the Jews?

Paul: In an uproar over Peter's escape! Herod had really botched things. He hurried to Caesarea, trying to distract the Jews by a show of power over the people of Tyre and Sidon.

Woman: How?

Paul: Well you see — Tyre and Sidon lay to the north — with one stroke, Herod Agrippa could cut off their food supplies from Palestine.

Woman: Oh — they needed his royal favor!

Paul: They did indeed. They arranged a huge festival — a circus they called it.

Woman: Political flattery —

Paul: Oh, indeed. On the second day of the festival, Herod entered the theatre clad in a robe of silver cloth. And when the sun glinted on his robe, the people cried out that he was a God!

Woman: Herod Agrippa would have loved that moment!

Paul: You picked the right word — it was but for the moment! Herod sickened and died.

Woman: Quickly?

Paul: Without warning. Just like that, the great adversary of the Christians vanished. Oh — there was great rejoicing in the church at Jerusalem.

Woman: You and Barnabas went back to Antioch?

Paul: And John Mark, too. Quite a different feeling from the last time I had left Jerusalem! This time, I went with such a light heart.

Woman: Why a light heart, Paul?

Paul: Peter was safe — the church secure. But most of all, the cancer of distrust that had eaten me up had been healed. After all those years of suspicion, I was free to work — to serve my Lord —

Woman: A chapter of your life closed behind you —

Paul: And a whole new chapter was about to open!

Woman: Thank you, Paul. We will talk again.

Dialogue 3
The First Missionary Journey

Woman: Well, Paul. I'm eager to hear of this new chapter in your life.

Paul: You mean, I suppose, my leaving Antioch.

Woman: Yes, the event that, in a historical sense, accounts for my being a Christian. Your first missionary journey!

Paul: *(laughing)* Well, we didn't call it that. You see, we didn't know there would be a second and a third!

Woman: You felt you could safely leave Antioch?

Paul: Oh, yes. A group of capable men had grown up in the church there — Lucius, who came from Cyrene in North Africa; Simeon, called Niger —

Woman: A Roman?

Paul: Yes — and there was Manean who had connections in the court of Herod.

Woman: Quite an international congregation!

Paul: A diverse group — unified in Christ, but conscious of the cultures they had come from.

Woman: Their own people — without the gospel.

Paul: Exactly. The Antioch church felt that Barnabas and I, with John Mark, should take the Gospel — move out from Antioch —

Woman: Where did you plan to go?

Paul: To the island of Cyprus.

Woman: Why Cyprus?

Paul: The Jewish Christians who first had preached in Antioch had come from Cyprus. Barnabas was a native of Cyprus. And it was only 50 miles away. A natural place to begin.

Woman: Let's see — you couldn't sail from Antioch itself, could you?

Paul: Oh no, no. Antioch was on the River Orontes, but inland — about 15 miles. We went down to Seleucia to wait.

Woman: Wait? Wait for what?

Paul: A cargo ship bound for Cyprus.

Woman: No passenger ships?

Paul: *(laughing)* You are spoiled! No, no passenger ships! And when a cargo ship finally did come, we had to wait all day while the goats were driven on board, the Syrian cows were tied under the deckway and the Arab horses going to Alexandria were tethered on the upper deck.

Woman: A regular Noah's ark! How did you three manage?

Paul: Late that night we walked into that inferno of smells, wrapped ourselves in blankets, and lay on the deck.

Woman: Could you sleep?

Paul: Barnabas and Mark slept, even with the hens and turkeys strolling around and over them. But I couldn't sleep. A long night. But gradually a gray light came; the stars faded. I got up and stood at the rail.

Woman: You could see Cyprus?

Paul: Like a shadow on the sea. And the lines of pink grew stronger and stronger. And then a burst of light!

Woman: A new dawn —

Paul: *(slowly)* Indeed, a new dawn.

Woman: Where did you land?

Paul: At Salamis, the commercial capital of the island. A lot of Jews lived there.

Woman: Business men?

Paul: Exporters — of oil and fruit — of wine and copper. All of them Jews.

Woman: So you were able to preach in synagogues?

Paul: Yes, but as in Antioch, mostly the God-fearers responded.

Woman: Did you stay in Salamis?

Paul: For quite a while. Then we walked to Paphos.

Woman: I think that's now called "Baffa." Why go there?

Paul: *(laughing)* No choice! Sergius Paulus sent for us.

Woman: And Sergius Paulus was — ?

Paul: The Roman governor of Cyprus — a man of learning, a contemporary of Pliny.

Woman: He wanted to hear you speak?

Paul: Evidently. But in his court, I clashed with a Jewish magician named Bar-Jesus.

Woman: What was a Jewish magician doing in a Roman governor's court?

Paul: Why, all the Roman dignitaries hired Jewish magicians — to interpret dreams — to cast spells —

Woman: And if Sergius Paulus believed your message — that day —

Paul: The day of Bar-Jesus was over! He tried hard to stop me from talking.

Woman: You faced him down?

Paul: Yes — until he crumpled like paper. A mist came over his eyes, and he was led away. Sergius Paulus believed!

Woman: So — the first Roman of high rank became a Christian! Did you keep on preaching to the Jews of Cyprus?

Paul: Yes — but soon I proposed to the others that we leave the island.

Woman: Why?

Paul: Cyprus was an out of the way place. I insisted we cross to the mainland of Asia Minor — to Perga in Pamphylia.

Woman: That city's now called "Eski-Kalesis," located on the southern tip of Turkey. What a big step to take!

Paul: *(short laugh)* A step that wasn't too popular with my companions, especially not with John Mark.

Woman: He wasn't too keen on this move into the Roman world?

Paul: That probably was part of his reluctance — Mark was a strict Jew. And he was a cousin of Barnabas —

Woman: Mark resented your taking over the leadership?

Paul: I think he may have — although Barnabas himself bore me no ill feeling. But most of all, John Mark was just a bit, uh, young.

Woman: Young?

Paul: Too young. Perhaps he was homesick. At any rate, to my disgust, Mark turned back to Jerusalem at Perga.

Woman: Did you preach at Perga?

Paul: No, *(sigh)* I fell ill. I had to get up higher onto the plateau. Perga was a malarial swamp.

Woman: That area is still noted for a particular strain of malaria — one with which you get headaches.

Paul: Like a red-hot thorn thrust through your forehead!

Woman: Since you fell ill, didn't it occur to you to go back with Mark?

Paul: *(vehemently)* Me? Turn back? Never!

Woman: I could have guessed that! Paul, you've told us about ship travel. On land, how did you go? I always think of you as walking.

Paul: I did walk sometimes.

Woman: But this time, in Perga, you were too ill to walk.

Paul: *(impatiently)* Yes, yes. I didn't have to walk. The Romans had built a network of modern roads all over the Roman empire. There were many ways to travel.

Woman: Such as — ?

Paul: There was a carriage, drawn by a horse, a two-wheeled affair called a *carpentium*. And there was a four horse coach called a *reda*.

Woman: That would be speedy — on the plains.

Paul: Over the mountain rocks, you often saw a *busternu*, a litter slung on shafts between two mules. We even had a sleeping carriage!

Woman: Very modern.

Paul: *(indignant)* In my day, the Eastern world was the modern world!

Woman: However you went out of Perga, it had to be at a snail's pace.

Paul: Yes. We crept up over the Taurus mountain to Pisidian Antioch.

Woman: I've often wondered — why two Antiochs?

Paul: *(laughing)* Two? There were 16 Antiochs scattered about the empire!

Woman: Why was that?

Paul: Roman soldiers, under Seleucius Nicator, had brought Roman law to the Galatian highlands. Seleucius named 16 cities in honor of his father, Antiochus!

Woman: How confusing!

Paul: *(laughing)* It was. To keep things clear, let's call this second Antioch — Pisidea!

Woman: A Roman colony, you say?

Paul: Yes. Often, as I lay awake at night, I heard the night watch giving its commands in Latin.

Woman: You recuperated there at Pisidia?

Paul: Yes — the air was dry and cool on that high plateau. As soon as I felt better, I began to preach.

Woman: In the synagogue?

Paul: Oh yes. The local Jews expected Palestinian Jews to speak to them. Besides, because they lived in the hinterlands, they were hungry for any word from Jerusalem.

Woman: And how did it go — what did you preach?

Paul: That the history of the Jews had culminated in Christ. And that most Jews were blind to that truth.

Woman: As you yourself had been. .

Paul: Indeed. As I had been. You see, Jews couldn't understand how God could hang on a cross. To the Jew, crucifixion meant a man had been cursed by God.

Woman: To hang on a cross then — meant that Jesus could not be God?

Paul: Yes. But I preached that the resurrection was proof that Jesus was God! He bore the shame. His purpose is undefeatable.

Woman: What else formed your Gospel, Paul?

Paul: That in Jesus Christ, men and women can find a forgiving power —

Woman: *(nodding)* A power that sets them free —

Paul: Free from the condemnation of the law, a law impossible for anyone to fulfill.

Woman: Were your sermons well-received?

Paul: Why, after a few weeks, almost the whole city was turning out — Jews, Romans, Greeks — even a few native-born Pisideans.

Woman: The Jewish leaders wouldn't care for that.

Paul: No. And they reacted by stirring up the non-Jewish women.

Woman: That seems strange. Why would non-Jewish women listen to Jewish leaders?

Paul: These God-fearing women loved the purity of ethic and the cleanliness of life in the Jewish religion. In the synagogue, they had taken refuge.

Woman: Refuge? From what?

Paul: From the sexual immorality of the pagan world. But the Jewish leaders persuaded these influential women that the new freedom I spoke of meant sexual license.

Woman: And yet these same Jews kept those same Gentile women in the outside court — looking in?

Paul: Yes. They didn't believe privilege was to be shared with Gentiles. Or with any woman! But in spite of the trouble, many Gentiles and Jews believed. After the church became established, we went eastward, about 90 miles along the Roman road to Iconium.

Woman: That's the modern city of Konya. And the same pattern developed there?

Paul: A little differently. The city split in two — but this time with Jews and Greeks on both sides. And a riot started!

Woman: Didn't the Roman soldiers step in?

Paul: Only a few were stationed there — not enough to stop the mob.

Woman: You got safely away?

Paul: Yes — to Lystra — a city about 18 miles farther east, a Roman city with a large garrison of soldiers.

Woman: A prudent move.

Paul: Well — it seemed so at the time. But I never did like being chased out of town! *(pause)* An odd thing happened in Lystra.

Woman: What was that?

Paul: *(laughing)* Barnabas and I were taken for the gods — Zeus and Hermes! They thought Barnabas was Zeus — naturally, they took me, the bald, bandy-legged, talkative man — for Hermes!

Woman: But why would they think you were gods?

Paul: We had cured a man, crippled from birth. And those simple people of Lystra knew an old story —

Woman: A legend?

Paul: Yes. Once, they said, Zeus and Hermes had come to earth in disguise. No one, except two old peasants, Philemon and his wife, Baucis, would take them in. The whole population, goes the tale, was wiped out — except for Philemon and Baucis.

Woman: Evidently the people of Lystra weren't going to make that mistake again! After you convinced them you were men, how did you preach to these pagan people? Jewish history would mean nothing to them.

Paul: I started with nature.

Woman: Oh. Because all people know about the rain and the sun and seed time and harvest?

Paul: Yes. And I went from those things to the living God who had made them.

Woman: A new approach for you.

Paul: A new approach for a new situation.

Woman: You stayed on in Lystra?

Paul: Long enough for Jews from Pisidia and Iconium to follow us —

Woman: Looking for more trouble?

Paul: Yes. And in Lystra, the Jews used a new approach too. They stirred up the rabble, telling them that the Jesus we preached was a man the Romans had seen fit to put to death! They came after us with stones.

Woman: Did you have any warning?

Paul: Not this time. The mob caught me when I was by myself. And they stoned me.

Woman: The very people who had hailed you as Hermes?

Paul: The very ones! And when they thought I was dead they dragged me out of the city to hide their crime from the Roman soldiers.

Woman: Where was Barnabas?

Paul: Trying to stop the mob. But he couldn't. Outside the city, he and a handful of believers formed a circle around me, protecting me.

Woman: Did they help you get away from Lystra?

Paul: When I could get to my feet, I went back to Lystra!

Woman: Paul!

Paul: I had to have my wounds cared for.

Woman: What if someone had seen you?

Paul: I intended them to see me. I wanted them to know that I, Paul, had not slunk away in the night.

Woman: But you did leave Lystra?

Paul: Yes. Openly and with dignity we went southeast to Derbe — about a day's journey.

Woman: You rested there?

Paul: I preached while my wounds healed. We had no trouble in Derbe.

Woman: That would be a pleasant change! Did you gain followers?

Paul: Many. After we had been there a good while, Barnabas and I decided we should go home.

Woman: How long had you been gone?

Paul: About two years. And there was no way to go further. Derbe was the last city on the Galatian plain, backed up against a snow-dusted mountain called Hoji Baba.

Woman: Then you would have to go back the way you had come?

Paul: Indeed yes. It would take amost a year to retrace our steps.

Woman: That could mean trouble.

Paul: Well, this time when we went back, we avoided the synagogues and met in the house churches of the Christians.

Woman: They had stayed together?

Paul: Yes. To help them, we chose, for each group, men we called elders.

Woman: To act as leaders?

Paul: Yes. We saw that the Christians must live in a disciplined fellowship.

Woman: There were to be no isolated, solitary Christians, then?

Paul: No indeed! There lay the danger! Some believers were Roman, some Greek, some Jew!

Woman: Widely different backgrounds.

Paul: Only a close fellowship in Christ could unite them. Barnabas and I saw that clearly. They had to love one another — in freedom. And that's what I wrote to all those churches in the Galatian highlands.

Woman: So, you made your way back through Lystra, Iconium, Pisidea — back down the Taurus mountain to Perga.

Paul: And this time, we preached in Perga.

Woman: Somehow, Paul, I thought you would. And from there you sailed back to Syria?

Paul: From the port of Attalia, yes.

Woman: You and Barnabas must have been glad to see Antioch!

Paul: There was a day of rejoicing with all the Christians. But when we told them of our journey and how many Gentiles and Jews had come to believe, they were sobered.

Woman: *(bewildered)* Why? Surely they were glad to hear that.

Paul: In a way, they were. But the mixture of Gentiles and Jews in the church, even at Antioch, was creating a real problem.

Woman: Between them and the Pharisees?

Paul: No — a problem within the church. No one knew what to require of the Gentiles. The question was: before a Gentile became a member of the Christian church, was it necessary that he should be circumcized?

Woman: Why was circumcision so important to the Jew?

Paul: Circumcision indicated a covenant with God, a sign in the man's flesh that he was willing to take upon himself the keeping of Jewish law.

Woman: What Antioch wanted to know was — must the Gentile, before he could become a Christian, first become a Jew?

Paul: Exactly.

Woman: What was the thinking of the mother church?

Paul: The Jerusalem church had always insisted upon circumcision for the Gentile. Antioch had not. Soon after we returned from overseas, some converted Pharisees from Jerusalem arrived in Antioch demanding we circumcize the Gentile Christians.

Woman: And you and Barnabas argued with them?

Paul: Indeed we did argue. But we both realized the problem could be settled only in the council at Jerusalem.

Woman: So you and Barnabas went to Jerusalem?

Paul: With Titus, a Greek Christian.

Woman: Do you remember the date of the council?

Paul: How could I forget it? It was the year 49 when we went to decide whether a man's salvation depended on faith in Christ or faith in Christ plus circumcision.

Woman: Did you, Paul, debate at the council?

Paul: I surely did. Vigorously. I cited how many uncircumcised Gentiles had believed in Cyprus and in the churches of Galatia. But it was Peter whose word carried the most weight.

Woman: Peter? The head of the Jewish church? Why would he argue for accepting the Gentiles as they were?

Paul: Because once when Peter was at Joppa staying with a tanner named Simon, he and Simon went up on the roof top. About noon it was.

Woman: Lunch time.

Paul: Peter was hungry and asked Simon for something to eat. And when Simon went below to make arrangements, Peter knelt to pray. And he saw, as he prayed, a sheet lowered. And in it all kinds of reptiles and animals and birds.

Woman: All unclean to the Jew?

Paul: *(with fervor)* Repulsive to the Jew. But a voice said, "Rise, Peter, kill and eat. What God has cleansed, you must not call unclean." That's why Peter, earlier, had agreed to baptize Cornelius!

Woman: Without requiring circumcision of him! I see, I see. The decision of the council was important!

Paul: Crucial! And even then, right there at the council, some die-hards challenged me. They tried to circumcize my Greek friend, Titus.

Woman: You didn't let them!

Paul: No indeed! I would not compromise the liberty we enjoyed in Christ. But it was quite a fight!

Woman: A real donny-brook at the first council! What was the final decision?

Paul: They set free the young church — free from Jewish law. The principle was clearly stated. *(pause)* But — as is often the case —

Woman: Practice didn't always follow principle?

Paul: Somehow, the principle did not carry over into actuality — not even with Peter!

Woman: That does surprise me!

Paul: When we went back to Antioch, Peter followed. He preached and taught and lived quite happily with the Gentile Christians until —

Woman: Until what?

Paul: Until some people sent by James visited Antioch and rebuked Peter for neglecting Jewish dietary laws.

Woman: And Peter didn't stand up to them?

Paul: No. He turned away from the Gentile Christians. And so did Barnabas! Imagine that. Barnabas!

Woman: Those men from Jerusalem must have put on considerable pressure.

Paul: They surely did. But I confronted Peter, showing him he had violated his own convictions.

Woman: You, Paul, publicly challenged Peter?

Paul: I had to. For the church, I had to.

Woman: Did Peter see where he was wrong?

Paul: Oh, yes. And Barnabas, too. But it was a touchy situation. And at a bad time, too.

Woman: How's that?

Paul: Well, we were planning our next missionary journey —

Woman: You and Barnabas were going?

Paul: *(hesitates)* Not together —

Woman: Oh? Why not?

Paul: We quarreled bitterly over John Mark. He wanted to go with us again.

Woman: You wouldn't take him?

Paul: *(stubbornly)* No one who had turned back once could go with me again.

Woman: You're a bit of a hard-head, Paul.

Paul: *(dryly)* So I've been told. At any rate, Barnabas and John Mark decided to go back to Cyprus together. I took Silas with me.

Woman: I don't believe you've mentioned Silas before, Paul.

Paul: Silas was a Jewish Christian, a member of the church at Jerusalem. He visited Antioch after the council meeting.

Woman: That choice seems rather surprising after the big dispute. But wait. Perhaps, through Silas, you wanted to verify for the Jerusalem church what was happening in the Gentile world?

Paul: *(short laugh)* That thought may have crossed my mind!

Woman: In your thinking, Paul, what was different this time as you prepared to leave Antioch?

Paul: This second time I saw so clearly that, to be a Christian, a Gentile need no longer stoop to enter the narrow door of the synagogue. Nor should he ever again be kept in the outer court of his faith!

Woman: The door of the Christian church, you believed, must be flung wide open to the world.

Paul: A world to be won for Christ — to be brought into a church set free from slavery to the Law!

Woman: Thank you, Paul. We shall talk again.

Dialogue 4

The Gospel
Reaches Europe

Woman: Well, Paul. This time when you, as an old hand, started out from Antioch with Silas, what was your itinerary?

Paul: First, we visited the churches of Asia Minor. Not Cyprus, though — Barnabas and John Mark went back there.

Woman: You and Silas, then, retraced your steps on the Galatian plains?

Paul: Yes. And at Lystra —

Woman: Oh yes! Where they had taken you for Hermes on your first journey!

Paul: *(laughing)* Yes. Much more satisfactory the second time — I found young Timothy there.

Woman: Timothy?

Paul: The child of a Jewish mother — and a Greek Father. *(abruptly)* I had Timothy circumcised.

Woman: Paul! You fought bitterly to keep Titus from being circumcized in Jerusalem!

Paul: That's right. No Greek believer was to be circumcized before baptism.

Woman: But you said Timothy's father was a Greek.

Paul: Exactly. To the Jew, the child of a mixed marriage was dead. Through that circumcision, I accepted, in front of all Jews, Timothy as a brother Jew — in fact — as my beloved son.

Woman: *(sighing)* Paul — your reasoning is always so involved.

Paul: *(sharply)* Timothy thought the same! There was no one whose mind worked so much like mine. I wanted him with me.

Woman: So Timothy went on with you and Silas?

Paul: Together, the three of us struck out into new territory — northwest — to the seacoast — to Alexandrian Troas, the city named for Alexander the Great.

Woman: *(nodding)* It's now called Eskistambul. A Roman colony then I suppose.

Paul: Of course. And there at Troas, Dr. Luke joined us.

Woman: Well! Your traveling party really picked up! You say Doctor Luke?

Paul: Luke was a physician. He was determined to take care of me!

Woman: He probably thought somebody should!

Paul: *(laughing)* Yes — I suppose so.

Woman: After Luke joined your party, where did you go?

Paul: We were most undecided there in Troas.

Woman: Why?

Paul: We had earlier wanted to go to Bithynia. But I felt uneasy — unsure —

Woman: So you didn't go to Bithynia?

Paul: No. Then, there in Troas where Alexander said his aim was to "marry the east to the west," I felt a new impulse toward making one world for Christ. In a dream, I saw a man beckoning me to come over to Macedonia.

Woman: Into Europe? And you responded?

Paul: As soon as we could, we set sail for Neapolis.

Woman: A town now called Kavalla.

75

Paul: From there we walked to Philippi, nine miles away.

Woman: That nine miles isn't exactly a stroll if I remember rightly. Between the coast and Philippi stands a mountain — Mount Symbolium.

Paul: Where the road twists up and up.

Woman: And slides down to an immense plain where Antony and Octavius defeated Brutus and Cassius.

Paul: *(approvingly)* You do know some ancient history! Did you also know that Antony settled most of the veterans from that battle in Philippi?

Woman: *(surprised)* No, I didn't. Lots of Romans then. Were there many Jews?

Paul: Very few. And no synagogue. But I managed to get into trouble anyway.

Woman: *(dryly)* Somehow I'm not surprised. How?

Paul: It all began quietly enough. In Philippi, that first Sunday, we preached along the river bank. There we met a woman named Lydia who believed and was baptized. Then she invited us to make her house our headquarters.

Woman: Without asking her husband? She sounds like an early women's libber!

Paul: Hmmm. I never heard that word! Lydia was a business-woman, a seller of purple cloth. Finally, after some urging, we accepted her invitation. But a few days later, on the way to her house, we passed a half-witted girl traveling with her Greek master.

Woman: *(bristling)* What do you mean her "master?"

Paul: She was his slave. You see, the Greeks believed in oracles — and this poor child babbled endlessly.

Woman: How could anyone understand her?

Paul: Her master interpreted her ravings.

Woman: For a fee I suppose.

Paul: Of course. And her master didn't take it kindly when in the name of Christ, I cured her.

Woman: You took away his livelihood — the man would be furious!

Paul: Indeed he was! He and some of his friends dragged Silas and me into the marketplace and whipped us —

Woman: *(horrified)* Why didn't you tell them you were a Roman citizen?

Paul: I thought of it, but I couldn't. You see — uh — Silas wasn't a Roman —

Woman: *(sighing)* After they whipped the two of you, did they let you go?

Paul: The Greek took us to the magistrates charging us with spreading doctrine unlawful for Romans to hear.

Woman: That's ridiculous.

Paul: *(nodding)* True. But Silas and I found ourselves in jail just the same!

Woman: An East European prisoner — terrible —

Paul: Worse than you can imagine. We were chained to the wall — and our feet fastened in stocks. Then, with wooden bars, they forced our legs as far apart as possible.

Woman: *(shocked)* That's inhuman!

Paul: That night an earthquake shook loose the bars. And our chains fell from the wall.

Woman: You could have walked out?

Paul: Yes. But we didn't.

Woman: *(puzzled)* Why not?

Paul: For one thing — the jailer —

Woman: *(bewildered)* Why would you care about the jailer?

Paul: It wasn't his fault we were there! He was on the point of killing himself. *(sternly)* Anyway, every person without Christ is of concern to me.

Woman: I'm sorry, Paul — I wasn't thinking.

Paul: That night, the jailer and his family believed in Jesus Christ. And we held a celebration — right there in the jail.

Woman: A funny place to celebrate.

Paul: *(laughing)* Yes, I suppose so. In the morning, I sent word through the jailer that I was a Roman citizen.

Woman: Then you left the jail?

Paul: *(short laugh)* That's what the magistrates hoped I would do. But I wouldn't leave until they came and apologized to me.

Woman: Paul, you are incredible.

Paul: They were frightened. Roman law forbade the flogging of a Roman citizen.

Woman: Were you able to start a church among the Philippians?

Paul: With three unlikely converts — Lydia, an Asiatic; the slave girl — a Greek, and the jailer — a Roman — we began the first Christian church in Europe.

Woman: It sounds as if you enjoyed Philippi.

Paul: I hated to leave. But I left Luke there — and other workers too. Timothy, Silas and I went on to Thessalonica.

Woman: About 100 miles away if you go through Amphipolis and Apollonia.

Paul: Yes — three days travel to Thessalonica —

Woman: Called Salonika now, I believe. A port city, isn't it?

Paul: Yes — the largest port on the Aegean Sea.

Woman: You had a place to stay?

Paul: Fortunately. We lodged with Jason, a fellow-countryman recently come to Thessalonica. A large Jewish community there.

Woman: So — you started off speaking in the synagogue —

Paul: Yes, but —

Woman: *(interrupting)* Yes, but the Jews grew restless!

Paul: *(short laugh)* A common pattern! They stirred up some agitators.

Woman: How?

Paul: In the Roman city, Jews lived as a rich minority. All the Jews had to do was hunt up some Roman rabble — give them my name — whisper treason — that was enough!

Woman: The mob came after you?

Paul: Right to Jason's house! But Silas and I weren't home. They took Jason to jail on charges of treason. That night, Timothy packed Silas and me off to Berea.

Woman: To what we now call Verria, about 40 miles southwest of Thessalonica. What happened to Jason?

Paul: When the magistrates discovered Jason was not Paul, they allowed him to post bond and go home. *(shaking his head)* After turning Jason's world upside down, I felt bad about going off to Berea.

Woman: Was everything all right in Berea?

Paul: Yes, a peaceful place. The Jews there were more than willing to hear me and to study the scriptures. But Timothy soon arrived to warn me that Jews from Thessalonica were on my heels.

Woman: You left Berea?

Paul: *(sighing)* Yes — Timothy escorted me south to Athens.

Woman: What about Silas?

Paul: Silas stayed behind in Berea. I sent Timothy back to him right away. Both of them returned to Thessalonica to help that infant church.

Woman: And you went to Athens. How?

Paul: We sailed from the coast of Thessaly.

Woman: A large ship?

Paul: No — small. We sailed so close to land I could smell the wild mint.

Woman: *(dreamily)* Athens — the name itself conjures up glories!

Paul: But even in my day — past glories.

Woman: Athens had lost first place to Rome?

Paul: Yes. Still, that first sight of Athens is — remarkable.

Woman: *(eagerly)* Tell me what you saw!

Paul: It was late afternoon. The sun was sinking behind the island of Aegina. And the slanting rays flashed gold —

Woman: Flashed gold?

Paul: From the gilded spear held high by Athena. And the last daylight warmed the slopes of Mount Hymettus.

Woman: And the city?

Paul: Brown and white houses. And on the Acropolis hill, the pillars of the Parthenon gleaming white.

Woman: And you, Paul, walked into Athens — the intellectual stronghold of the Roman empire.

Paul: Into a city filled with students, some of them reading books, but most of them talking — talking — talking!

Woman: Discussing philosophy?

Paul: The streets rang with the arguments of the Platonists, the Stoics, the Epicureans! Reminded me of my boyhood days in Tarsus.

Woman: You joined the throngs?

Paul: I walked the streets of Athens — everywhere marble temples, statues to every known god. *(short laugh)* Even one to an unknown god!

Woman: *(laughing)* To an unknown god?

Paul: The story goes that about 600 years before my time, a plague struck Athens. The people sacrificed to all the gods. But —

Woman: The plague continued?

Paul: No let-up at all. Then the Cretan prophet, Epimenides, drove a flock of black and white sheep to the Areopagus —

Woman: *(nodding)* The meeting place —

Paul: There the sheep stopped. And there they were sacrificed to the unknown god.

Woman: And the plague ended?

Paul: Yes. So they erected a statue there in the Areopagus — where I was invited to speak.

Woman: The Athenians invited you, a Jewish stranger — to speak?

Paul: *(dryly)* The Athenians loved to hear anything new, a curiosity mingled with intellectual arrogance.

Woman: How did you begin, Paul? The Athenians had no Jewish background; yet they weren't simple like the peasants of Lystra.

Paul: I pointed at the altar to the unknown god and declared who that God was.

Woman: They listened?

Paul: As long as I stayed with philosophical truths!

Woman: When did they grow restless?

Paul: When I spoke of the resurrection of Christ —

Woman: The core of the Christian faith —

Paul: Always a stumbling block to the Jews — and but foolishness to the Greek!

Woman: Did the Athenians get angry?

Paul: *(shaking his head)* Athenians are much too sophisticated. Anger would have been easier to swallow than their amused tolerance.

Woman: Paul, you could not know it, but the day would come when the Greek Parthenon would be consecrated to that Christ you declared.

Paul: That consoles me. I considered myself a failure in Athens.

Woman: You didn't stay long, then?

Paul: Only a short while. And only a few converts. I went on to Corinth where I arranged to meet Silas and Timothy.

Woman: Let's see. Corinth lies west of Athens on a narrow isthmus —

Paul: The isthmus that joins the Peloponnesus to the Greek mainland.

Woman: You went overland then —

Paul: Yes. Over beyond Megara where the road runs up and down on the edge of the Scironian rocks.

Woman: I remember! A scary road!

Paul: A sheer drop to the sea! But the road at last straightened out. Corinth sits on a long, undulating plateau, dominated by a huge mountain.

Woman: The Areo-Corinth. Paul, I notice that you almost always went to seaports or crossroad cities. Was that a deliberate policy?

Paul: Not at first. Certainly not in Cyprus. But after that — yes. Look at the possibilities in Corinth — two harbors — the eastern one packed with Egyptian, Asiatic and Phoenician galleys —

Woman: And the western one docking ships from Italy, Spain and the Adriatic!

Paul: And if we carried out our work well — the seed of the Gospel — cargo in all of them.

Woman: Still, Paul — by their very nature, these cities are — well —

Paul: Go on — say it — cesspools. Corinth the worst of all. In earlier centuries, it was infamous for the temple of Aphrodite —

Woman: So rank that even the Romans, who had few moral scruples, destroyed it!

Paul: Yes — about 150 years before my time. But the reputation lingered. In fact, the Corinthians took a perverse pride in their wickedness. Frankly, I was in no mood for Corinth!

Woman: That doesn't sound like you, Paul.

Paul: Perhaps not. But when I got to Corinth, I felt suddenly — old. My eyes had grown weaker; my body was scarred by the stones of Lystra —

Woman: And the whips of Philippi —

Paul: And the stocks! More than that — I seemed depressed. I hadn't liked being hustled out of Thessalonica. And I could still hear the laughter of the Athenians mocking my words. I was so weak in body and spirit that I trembled. No, I was in no mood for Corinth!

Woman: What about Timothy and Silas?

Paul: *(irritated)* They weren't in Corinth when I got there!

Woman: So, you didn't plan to stay?

Paul: I certainly did not. I wanted to go back to Thessalonica. But my money was all gone. *(shaking head)* I don't know what I would have done without Priscilla and Aquila.

Woman: Christians?

Paul: Jewish Christians. From Rome.

Woman: Rome! Why would they leave Rome for a hole like Corinth?

Paul: *(dryly)* Not their idea! In 49, the Emperor Claudius had thrown all the Christians out of Rome!

Woman: Why?

Paul: He got tired of the constant squabbles between Jews and Christians. *(laughing)* Though he didn't mean to, Claudius had sent me friends!

Woman: You stayed with Priscilla and Aquila?

Paul: Yes. I worked with Aquila. He made tent cloth.

Woman: Corinth needed tents?

Paul: Not many. But they did need sails.

Woman: I hate to be critical of your new friends, Paul. But there you were — preaching, teaching, writing letters to the other churches. *(rising indignation)* How could Priscilla and Aquila allow you to waste your failing eyesight on — on sail cloth! How could they?

Paul: You don't understand. On my journeys, I never took money from the people among whom I worked.

Woman: Why not? Isn't a laborer worthy of his hire?

Paul: Absolutely. But, in the Gentile world, a teacher lived on the fees of his students. His teaching was a money-making business.

Woman: Oh — you didn't want that kind of relationship with believers —

Paul: Indeed not! But — if an established church, as it grew, wished to send me money — that I accepted gratefully.

Woman: Each church, then, could have a part in spreading the Gospel.

Paul: Exactly. Exactly.

Woman: Corinth would seem to have been an impossible place for the Gospel!

Paul: I would have said the same. But, among the Gentiles, the church in Corinth grew vigorously — even exuberantly!

Woman: And the Jews?

Paul: Same as always. When I preached, they called out, "Anathema Jesus!"

Woman: You argued with them?

Paul: I was through arguing. I shook off the dust of my robes and left the synagogue behind.

Woman: The Jews, then, to follow Jesus, also had to leave the synagogue?

Paul: Many of them did just that. Including Crispus, the ruler of the synagogue. I baptized him myself.

Woman: How that must have shaken the Jewish community! Where did Christians meet?

Paul: Right next door to the synagogue. At the home of Titus Justus — a Roman.

Woman: After you moved into the house church, did the Jews let you alone?

Paul: Not at all. Not at all. They waited patiently for the right moment!

Woman: And when did that moment arrive?

Paul: In 52, when the Roman Senate appointed Junius Gallio Annaeus as proconsul to Corinth.

Woman: That's when the Jews made their move?

Paul: They organized a riot designed to strike fear to the heart of the new consul — and hauled me into his court.

Woman: On what charge?

Paul: Persuading people to worship God contrary to Mosaic law.

Woman: Scarcely a charge to be heard in a Roman court!

Paul: Gallio would have agreed with you. He saw at once he had been duped.

Woman: He told the crowd so?

Paul: He threw everyone out! Before I could stop them, friends of Crispus beat up Sosthenes, the new leader of the synagogue.

Woman: I'd say it served him right!

Paul: *(dryly)* You sound like one of my Corinthian church members.

Woman: *(taken aback)* I do?

Paul: Sometimes I doubted they would ever understand!

Woman: Well, no one reading your letters could doubt your love for them —

Paul: I'm glad for that.

Woman: How long did you stay in Corinth?

Paul: About a year and a half. Finally, Timothy and Silas arrived, bringing encouragement from Thessalonica. Like a tonic to me, it was. I was able to settle down contentedly to my teaching. And then, the next spring, the three of us started home, along with Priscilla and Aquila.

Woman: Priscilla and Aquila went to Antioch?

Paul: No, No. We left them at Ephesus.

Woman: But you didn't stay in Ephesus?

Paul: Not on that trip. I did preach in the synagogue there and promised to come back if I could. But I yearned to get back to Jerusalem for the feast of Pentecost.

Woman: You needed a renewal of spirit.

Paul: Indeed. All my reserves were depleted.

Woman: No wonder. You had been gone three years —

Paul: And covered about 2,800 miles —

Woman: More than the first journey —

Paul: Almost twice as many.

Woman: You had crossed many boundaries —

Paul: Not only the boundaries of Israel but the boundaries of Asia —

Woman: You had burst open the closed world of nations —

Paul: And some day — some day I knew I would go to Rome! Some day the Gospel would be preached to the ends of the world!

Woman: But for your day —

Paul: For my day, with these crossings of boundaries, I, Paul, had set free the mystery of the Gospel — in the rumbling, stirring continent of Europe!

Woman: Thank you, Paul. We will talk again.

Dialogue 5
The Third Journey And Trials In Caesarea

Woman: Paul, after you came home from your second journey, did you visit Jerusalem?

Paul: Once, but only briefly. Antioch, not Jerusalem, had become my Christian home.

Woman: You stayed a while in Antoich?

Paul: More than a year — from the autumn of 52 to the spring of 54.

Woman: And then — off again?

Paul: *(nodding)* Timothy and I systematically revisited many of the Asian churches, picking up Titus on our way. And then, the three of us, went on to Ephesus.

Woman: Oh, where you had left Priscilla and Aquila!

Paul: Yes. Bless them, they had been preparing for me. A good job they did too! I stayed there in Ephesus for three years.

Woman: Well, that's a change — isn't it?

Paul: Hmmm, yes. As you know, on the first journey — and on the second as well — we moved from place to place.

Woman: *(dryly)* And sometimes you were moved!

Paul: *(laughing)* Usually before I was ready. But in Corinth, because I had been forced to wait over the winter for Timothy and Silas —

Woman: You saw some value in a longer stay?

Paul: I seemed to need more and more time to think about all the infant churches. *(sighing)* Especially those Corinthians!

Woman: Had they swung back toward paganism?

Paul: They surely had. I tried to remember how hard it would be for those ordinary men and women, nobodies really, to live a pure life in the midst of a monstrous society. But their sin was so flagrant — I had to write —

Woman: And after your letter, did they mend their ways?

Paul: No! They didn't like what I said at all. Then, I heard from Chloe's people. They told of more corruption and immorality and scandal at Corinth. I wrote another letter and sent it with Timothy.

Woman: We have that letter, Paul. But because we don't have the first one, we call it 1 Corinthians. Did the second letter help matters?

Paul: No — not at all!

Woman: Well, what more could you do?

Paul: Well, I had to try. I made a hasty visit to Corinth from Ephesus, a painful visit — accomplished nothing. In fact, I made things worse!

Woman: So you came back to Ephesus — ?

Paul: *(nodding)* In anguish over the Corinthians. With many tears, I wrote another letter — a severe one — and sent it — this time with Titus. *(aggrieved)* Titus got on much better with them than I.

Woman: *(hastily)* Well, Paul, when many people become involved with a congregation, people make — comparisons —

Paul: Yes — Corinth had Stephanus and Apollos and Timothy and Titus — good men. *(bursting out)* But I was an apostle! I bore scars for them in my body!

Woman: *(trying to change subject)* Paul, why don't you tell me about Ephesus?

Paul: *(sighing)* All right. Ephesus was a wealthy city — the capital of Asia.

Woman: Ah — an important city —

Paul: Yes, but a hard city for the Gospel — why, in Ephesus boiled a cauldron of magic!

Woman: You had run into magic before, hadn't you? Bar Jesus — at the court of Sergius Paulus — and that demented slave girl in Philippi —

Paul: But those were isolated cases. This magic pervaded the whole city — a black magic associated with the goddess Artemis.

Woman: The Artemis of the Greeks? The virgin huntress?

Paul: The Artemis of Ephesus was far from virginal! More a goddess from antiquity, sculpted in dark marble — a many-breasted goddess, her upper body studded with bees.

Woman: A fertility goddess then —

Paul: *(nodding)* Each spring, May, a month of games was held in her honor. The revelers thronged into Ephesus.

Woman: *(short laugh)* Sounds like our Mardi Gras — noise — drunkenness — day and night —

Paul: Indeed. Aquila and I, after working all day, would try to sleep. But the streets rang with shouts, *(shouting)* "Great is Artemis of the Ephesians!" And the women — poor things — would be dragged through the streets, subjected to the grossest sexual perversions.

Woman: I'm glad you brought up that subject, Paul.

Paul: *(bewildered)* What subject?

Woman: Women. Some people today call you a male chauvinist.

Paul: *(bewildered)* A what?

Woman: A man who, uh, uh, well, keeps a woman in her "place" — in slang — a pig!

Paul: They call me that? Why — the women of Corinth and Ephesus were treated like animals — worse than animals!

Woman: Why did you tell the women in the church not to wear make-up and jewelry?

Paul: Because the prostitutes at the temple of Artemis wore make-up and jewelry!

Woman: And the veil?

Paul: A woman without a veil — was — nothing! Any man felt free to insult her or assault her!

Woman: That's hard for a 20th century woman to understand.

Paul: I suppose it is. In my day, however, the veil conveyed honor and dignity upon the woman. With it, she could go anywhere — she could take her rightful place in the church.

Woman: *(sarcastic)* Really? How about your telling women to keep silent in church?

Paul: I encouraged women to pray in church. But if either a Greek or a Jewish woman had tried to speak or teach, she would have been humiliated.

Woman: Why?

Paul: Sophocles had taught that "Silence confers grace upon a woman." And Rabbinical teachings simply forbade a woman to speak in public.

Woman: Well, there's another charge they lay to you today. When you were listing the post-resurrection appearances, you left out Mary.

Paul: Yes, yes I did. I was arguing. And women were not, in Jewish law, considered to be legal witnesses. If I had included Mary, I would have weakened, not strengthened, my case.

Woman: Let me understand this. What you did, Paul, was to take first century customs and values and apply them to specific situations in the church?

Paul: Of course! The first century is the one I lived in!

Woman: *(suspiciously)* You weren't trying to downgrade women?

Paul: *(indignant)* Downgrade? I taught that there must be no distinction between male and female — both are one in Christ. I taught that in marriage the man and woman must live in mutual equality. Why — I loved Timothy's mother Eunice, and his grandmother, Lois!

Woman: *(grudgingly)* I know you admired Lydia.

Paul: Yes — what did you call her — a woman's libber? And then, of course there was Phoebe and Priscilla, my fellow workers. And in Rome, later on, Junia was a fellow prisoner — a fellow apostle. These women were the best!

Woman: *(embarrassed)* I'm glad we talked about you — and women, Paul —

Paul: (sighing) It seems I am destined to be misunderstood — even in your day.

Woman: *(briskly)* How did you combat the worship of Artemis?

Paul: Head on.

Woman: That sounds like you, Paul.

Paul: *(laughing)* You're probably right. I moved nearer the temple of Artemis — into the lecture hall of Tyrannus — where the Ephesians gathered.

Woman: And they noticed you?

Paul: They noticed me all right — especially the silversmiths.

Woman: Why especially the silversmiths?

Paul: They sold souvenirs — silver miniatures of the temple of Artemis.

Woman: And right there within sight of her pavilion, you preached against false gods?

Paul: *(nodding)* Month by month, year by year, the silversmiths' business fell off. They hated me. That third year while Titus was gone —

Woman: To Corinth, you mean — ?

Paul: Yes. In the spring, just before the big festival, Demetrius —

Woman: One of the silversmiths?

Paul: Their leader. He roused his fellow workers, and one morning, they rushed out of their workshops to the great theater. On their way, they seized two of my companions, Gaius and Aristarchus.

Woman: Were you preaching that morning?

Paul: I was at home. I heard the rioters, some shouting one thing, some another. I started to the hall, but my friends stopped me.

Woman: Probably a good thing too —

Paul: Half of the mob didn't know what was going on. The Jews — afraid the riot would turn against them — sent up a spokesman named Alexander —

Woman: Did he quiet the mob?

Paul: As soon as they saw he was a Jew, the silversmiths hauled him down.

Woman: Getting dangerous —

Paul: Then the town clerk of Ephesus, a Roman, mounted the stage and just stood there — his arms folded.

Woman: Ah —

Paul: Silence fell. In a cold voice, the Roman pointed out that the supremacy of Artemis was not in question, that the Christians had neither robbed the temple nor blasphemed the goddess.

Woman: Did his logic prevail?

Paul: *(short laugh)* Coupled with his threat to call in the Roman army — yes!

Woman: So the danger was over.

Paul: Temporarily. But I saw I had put my friends in mortal danger. It was time for me to leave Ephesus.

Woman: Without Titus?

Paul: I arranged to meet him in Philippi. And when he came there, he brought news from Corinth.

Woman: Good news or bad news?

Paul: Good news! They wanted me to come!

Woman: And you went?

Paul: Not before I wrote a letter of reconciliation. I wanted to be sure I was welcome!

Woman: That's your fourth letter to Corinth — two have been lost, Paul. We call your fourth letter, 2 Corinthians. When you got there, were they happy to see you?

Paul: Titus had done a fine job. I had a wonderful, precious time in Corinth.

Woman: A change had come over them?

Paul: Over them, over me too. I knew I would never be back again.

Woman: That's when differences have a tendency to melt away —

Paul: *(nodding)* I shared with them my dreams of going to Rome. In the spring of 58 I had written the Christians in Rome to tell them my plan.

Woman: But first you had to go home.

Paul: But not empty-handed. I saw to it that the Gentile churches took up a collection for the poor of Jerusalem.

Woman: Heaping coals?

Paul: Well — the poor of Jerusalem certainly needed help. But I did think the gifts from Gentile Christians might help relationships!

Woman: Did you go by ship from Corinth to Syria?

Paul: We intended to. But when we saw the ship was loaded with Jewish pilgrims going to Jerusalem for the Passover —

Woman: You feared a plot?

Paul: Unfortunately, yes. We changed our plans and went overland.

Woman: You say "we." Who?

Paul: Disciples from Berea, Thessalonica, Derbe and Ephesus.

Woman: Why so many?

Paul: Men charged with collecting the money. I met Luke in Philippi. He and I spent Passover there while the others went on. We caught up with them at Troas.

Woman: Did you stay there?

Paul: Only a week — but a week I won't forget.

Woman: What happened?

Paul: I was preaching one night — *(laughing a little)* and a young man named Eutychus —

Woman: I know that story — he was sitting in a window —

Paul: *(laughing)* And I preached on and on — Eutychus fell asleep!

Woman: And fell two stories to the ground!

Paul: Everyone thought he had been killed! I ran down the stairs and put my arms around him, heaving a sigh of relief when he started to breathe again!

Woman: That incident has been of no small comfort to generations of preachers!

Paul: *(dryly)* I'm sure it has!

Woman: But why did you preach so long, Paul?

Paul: Because I was leaving the next morning. I taught all that night. Next morning, I walked to Assas, a town about 30 miles away. Luke and the others went to Assas, too, but by ship — around Cape Lectum.

Woman: *(bewildered)* Why did they go by ship?

Paul: They were carrying a large chest of money. And I needed time alone to — to deal with my forebodings of disaster.

Woman: Disaster? Waiting for you in Jerusalem?

Paul: Undoubtedly — waiting for me.

Woman: I see. At Assas, they took you on board and went on to Syria?

Paul: Not directly. We skirted the coast of Asia minor from Cheos to Samoa. And then we stopped at Miletus.

Woman: Why?

Paul: I had sent word for the elders of Ephesus to meet me there — it would be safe.

Woman: It's hard to say good-bye to friends.

Paul: *(puzzled)* You know the elders of Ephesus wept and kissed me —

Woman: Why should that surprise you? You loved them, didn't you?

Paul: Oh yes, yes. But I had been so stern with them. I hadn't realized —

Woman: That they loved you?

Paul: *(nodding)* It's hard for an old fighter to defend himself against love. I was overwhelmed. And every place we stopped — at the island of Rhodes, on the beach at Tyre and at Caesarea where we lodged with Philip — the same thing!

Woman: Did others sense trouble was coming?

Paul: Everywhere! Philip's daughter prophesied. And a prophet named Agabus took my cloak and tied up his hands, saying I would be bound over to the Gentiles!

Woman: But you went on.

Paul: *(struggling)* No choice. Ahead of me — in Jerusalem — lay my destiny.

Woman: How were things, politically, when you arrived in Jerusalem?

Paul: Tense. The nation teetered on the brink of chaos. Hatred of Roman rule boiled over. Riots started. And the Roman Senate posted Felix to Jerusalem.

Woman: Was Felix able to restore order?

Paul: No. In fact, under a so-called prophet from Egypt, a mob attacked Jerusalem. Felix called out the infantry — many, many Jews were killed.

Woman: No wonder the country was tense. Were the Christians glad to see you?

Paul: We were received warmly. There was so much suffering — we were glad we had brought the money.

Woman: But the apostles — did they welcome you? How about James?

Paul: *(hesitating)* James was worried. I had with me Greeks and Romans, Gentile Christians. And during the riot Gentiles had killed Jews.

Woman: James considered your presence to be a threat?

Paul: *(nodding)* James counseled me to take the Nazarite vow.

Woman: *(puzzled)* What's the Nazarite vow?

Paul: A Jewish rite. The man shaves his head and spends seven days in ceremonial purification within the temple.

Woman: You agreed to that, Paul?

Paul: *(short laugh)* I even agreed to pay expenses, not only for myself, but for four other of my companions.

Woman: Why would you put yourself through such a rite?

Paul: I would have done almost anything to reconcile Gentiles and Jews. Otherwise, nothing but bloodshed lay ahead between brothers in Christ!

Woman: And so you had your head shaved. Did it help?

Paul: *(ruefully)* Something went wrong. On the seventh day, to see Trophemus, one of my Ephesian converts, I stepped out —

Woman: What do you mean, "stepped out?" Out of the temple?

Paul: Out of the inner sanctuary — into the court of the Gentiles.

Woman: And someone saw you, with your shaven head, talking to a Gentile?

Paul: Yes. Some Asian Jews there for Passover — Jews who had harassed me on my journeys — they shouted out that I had taken a Gentile into the sanctuary!

Woman: I can imagine what happened with feelings running so high!

Paul: Everyone grabbed at me. I struggled to get back into the sanctuary.

Woman: Did the priests inside help?

Paul: *(short laugh)* They put their shoulders to the great doors of Corinthian bronze and slammed them in my face.

Woman: *(shocked)* And left you at the mercy of the mob?

Paul: I was dragged down under many feet. Then I heard the Roman guard clatter into the court of the Gentiles.

Woman: *(surprised)* Where did they come from?

Paul: Down the steps leading into the temple from the fortress of Antonia.

Woman: The soldiers rescued you?

Paul: They thrust through the crowd with spears and shields, lifted me and carried me on their shoulders back the way they had come.

Woman: And when they reached the steps?

Paul: They set me down. When the mob surged forward, the soldiers crossed spears in front of me. I gasped out some words in Greek to Lysias, their commander.

Woman: That must have startled him.

Paul: He had thought I was that Egyptian who had led the big riot.

Woman: Why would he think that?

Paul: The Egyptian had just escaped. That's why Lysias had his soldiers on alert. I told them I was a Jew and asked if I could speak to the people in Aramaic.

Woman: Did he allow that?

Paul: He thought it would quiet them down. I tried to explain my Christian ties with the Greeks and the Romans. But when I said, "Gentile," the mob howled.

Woman: Lysias wouldn't have any idea what you said. I bet he got angry!

Paul: Oh yes. He had the soldiers haul me away.

Woman: Into the barracks of Antonia?

Paul: Yes — where Lysias ordered the centurion to beat the truth out of me. As the man raised his whip, I asked if it was lawful to flog a Roman citizen.

Woman: I imagine that shook him up.

Paul: He dropped his whip! There I was, a Jew with a shaven head, speaking Latin, claiming to be a Roman citizen!

Woman: No wonder he dropped the whip! What did he do?

Paul: Like any good soldier, he took his problem higher up — back to Lysias.

Woman: The Greek?

Paul: Greek, yes. Also a Roman citizen. He told me he had bought his citizenship. I told him I was free-born.

Woman: That impressed him?

Paul: Surely. The next day he went with me to the Sanhedrin. He saw the high priest hit me in the mouth. Lysias hauled me out of there because the Pharisees and the Sadducees started to fight.

Woman: Why would Jew fight Jew?

Paul: I started it when I spoke of the resurrection. The Pharisees believed in the resurrection. But the Sadducees did not.

Woman: You were fast becoming what we call a hot potato.

Paul: Exactly! In a couple of days, the Jews asked for me to be brought again before the Sanhedrin. But my nephew came to the barracks and told Lysias that 40 men waited to kill me, wanting only a promise of no interference from him.

Woman: Lysias couldn't risk having a Roman citizen killed by Jews!

Paul: That night he sent me off to Caesarea with a letter to Felix.

Woman: Under guard?

Paul: Two hundred soldiers, 70 horsemen and 200 spearmen!

Woman: That's a small army!

Paul: At Antipatris the danger was over — all but the calvary returned to Jerusalem.

Woman: At Caesarea, where did they put you?

Paul: In prison at Herod's palace.

Woman: After you were out of Jerusalem, did the Jews drop the matter?

Paul: Not a chance. Five days later, a party came for my trial before Felix. Their lawyer, Tertullus, twisting the truth, painted me as a dangerous agitator.

Woman: But you had been in Jerusalem only 12 days! Where would they scrape up such evidence?

Paul: They couldn't. So Felix adjourned the trial.

Woman: Adjourned? Why not dismissed?

Paul: Felix was afraid of the Jews.

Woman: *(shaking her head)* So, he kept you in prison?

Paul: *(nodding)* But he often sent for me — each time, he wanted — a bribe.

Woman: How long did he keep up that cat and mouse game?

Paul: Two years. And then riots started again — all over the nation.

Woman: Bad news for Rome.

Paul: Bad news for Felix, too. The new emperor, Nero, wanted no trouble in the hinterlands!

Woman: Nero removed Felix from office?

Paul: Yes. But — for spite — Felix left me in jail. Then Porcius Festus, the new consul, arrived from Rome.

Woman: And the Jews saw another opportunity to get you?

Paul: They gave Festus a big welcome in Jerusalem. And persuaded him I should be sent back to them.

Woman: For another trial before the Sanhedrin?

Paul: Yes. But my nephew slipped me the word I was to be assassinated on the way.

Woman: It seems all the cards had been played out.

Paul: Not quite. I had one more. I appealed to Caesar.

Woman: A formal request as a Roman citizen for a trial in Rome?

Paul: *(nodding)* My trump card!

Woman: Festus sent you to Rome?

Paul: Not before we played one more charade — a so-called trial before Herod Agrippa.

Woman: The same Herod Agrippa who had killed the disciple James?

Paul: No. Herod Agrippa II, son of that murderer. Herod and his sister, Bernice, making a courtesy call on Festus, decided they wanted to hear me speak.

Woman: A royal whim?

Paul: One that occasioned a royal spectacle. Into the palace chamber marched the military guard. Festus in his scarlet cloak! The local dignitaries in their best finery!

Woman: *(short laugh)* What! No trumpets?

Paul: Trumpets too! And then Bernice, a great beauty, entered on the arm of her brother. Festus seated them on his royal throne. Black slaves waved ostrich feathers above their royal heads.

Woman: Quite a show! But you were no stranger to command performances. In Cyprus you stood before Sergius Paulus; in Corinth, before Gallio —

Paul: And Felix. And Festus. And now before a king — Agrippa!

Woman: *(dryly)* And all remembered only because you, Paul, stood before them. What did you tell Herod and Bernice?

Paul: My life story. When I spoke of the resurrection, I was overcome with passion. And Festus cried out, "Paul, you are mad."

Woman: And Agrippa?

Paul: He drawled, "You almost persuade me to be a Christian." Showing off he was.

Woman: A bit hard to take, I should think.

Paul: I burst out, "I would to God that all who hear me this day were persuaded to be like me."

Woman: Except for your chains.

Paul: I wouldn't wish those chains on anybody. But Herod Agrippa got in the last word. He rose and yawned and said to Festus, "Pity. The man might have been set at liberty if he had not appealed to Caesar."

Woman: What a cruel jest!

Paul: He didn't bother me. God had been planning for years to send me to Rome.

Woman: But you were going in chains!

Paul: Yes. In chains. But I, Paul, would go to the heart of the Roman empire — a free man in Jesus Christ!

Woman: Then God, not Agrippa, had the last word. Thank you, Paul. We will talk again.

Dialogue 6
Journey To Rome
– Paul's Last Days

Woman: So Paul, it was Festus and Agrippa who sent you off on your fourth journey.

Paul: *(nodding)* With Aristarchus — a Christian from Thessalonica. And, of course, Luke went with me.

Woman: What a comfort he must have been! Were you kept locked up?

Paul: At times. But especially on shipboard, Julius, the centurion, ordered the soldiers to let us walk about freely.

Woman: You sailed directly to Rome?

Paul: Oh no, no. That was impossible! We sailed up the coast, from Caesarea to Sidon. And then we headed north, slipping under the island of Cyprus.

Woman: Seeing Cyprus must have brought back memories.

Paul: It did indeed. The first foray into Cyprus with Barnabas seemed long, long before.

Woman: You said you were going north? Why not west? That's where Rome lies.

Paul: *(impatiently)* I told you — it was impossible. We had a one-masted ship and a square sail. We couldn't make headway against the prevailing west wind. And after rounding Cyprus, we landed at Myra.

Woman: In Lycia, on the coast of Asia Minor? That is out of the way.

Paul: *(very patiently)* But the city of Alexandria lies almost directly south. Ships, carrying wheat from Egypt to Italy, stopped in Myra on the way to Rome. Julius hurried us onto one of those.

Woman: What time of the year, Paul?

Paul: Autumn, with bad weather coming on. That's why the centurion rushed us on board.

Woman: Your ship was not equipped for winter?

Paul: The ship was fairly small, no rudder — just two side paddles. Even if the ship had been a better one, it wasn't safe to travel in winter — with the coasts not lighted, the reefs not marked.

Woman: About how many of your party came on board, Paul?

Paul: About 100 crewmen and 100 soldiers.

Woman: And prisoners?

Paul: Seventy.

Woman: Two hundred seventy besides the crew on a small ship! And a cargo of grain as well! How did the voyage go?

Paul: Not well. Not well at all. Even along the southern coast of Asia Minor, we could only crawl. Two weeks later we were just off the port of Cnidus.

Woman: I see. You sailed between the mainland and the island of Rhodes. And you landed at Cnidus?

Paul: No. We turned south, and, before a furious wind, ran for the shelter of Crete. In the lee of the island, we were able to limp into the tiny harbor of Fairhaven.

Woman: Well named, Paul.

Paul: Indeed, yes. Julius called a council to decide whether to harbor there for the winter or to go on. He asked me to join the ship's officers.

Woman: *(surprised)* He invited you, a prisoner, to sit at the council? Why?

Paul: Because of my experience with the sea.

Woman: Of course! You had sailed those waters for many years! What opinion did you offer?

Paul: I advised the council to keep the ship in Fairhaven until spring.

Woman: And the ship's officers?

Paul: They wanted to go farther north along the island to Phoenice, a more commodius harbor and a much larger city.

Woman: And Julius took their advice?

Paul: Well, the day of the council the sun shone and a deceptive wind blew from the sea. Made their plan seem easy.

Woman: So you sailed from Fairhaven with the wind behind you?

Paul: Yes. But at Cape Matala, the Euroclydon rushed down on us.

Woman: You mean the wind changed direction?

Paul: Completely. The gale came from north and east. Blew us south — the captain maneuvered the ship behind a small island — one named Cauda —

Woman: Cauda? Oh yes, yes — we call it Gaudos —

Paul: While the ship lay in the shelter of Cauda, the captain ordered the crew to frap the ship.

Woman: Frap? I don't know that word.

Paul: The ship's timbers had started to split. The men passed hausers beneath the hull and tightened them with a winch —

Woman: I see — they wrapped the ship up — like a package.

Paul: Yes — a last ditch effort to hold the ship together. The crew finished the job just as we passed the island.

Woman: Could the captain hold course?

Paul: No. We scudded before the wind, driven further south toward the Syrtis Sands.

Woman: The Syrtis Sands?

Paul: Sands off North Africa, the graveyard of many a ship. The captain struck sail and locked the paddles.

Woman: So the ship would drift?

Paul: Exactly. But, in the heavy weather, we were being swamped. On the second day, we threw the tackle overboard. On the third day, every spare piece of gear.

Woman: You say "we?"

Paul: In the storm all of us — soldiers — prisoners — crew — worked together for our salvation.

Woman: How long did the storm last?

Paul: For two weeks we saw neither the sun nor the moon.

Woman: And the soldiers and crew?

Paul: They clung to the sides of the ship, so sick and frightened they couldn't eat.

Woman: And you, Paul?

Paul: I spoke to them, moving around among them, trying to comfort them, urging them to hang on.

Woman: Weren't you afraid?

Paul: Well, yes and no. Fury like that strikes fear into every one. On the other hand, I was confident God meant me to fulfill my appeal to Caesar.

Woman: But the ship must have been in desperate straits!

Paul: *(nodding)* Day after day we drifted helplessly in the Adriatic.

Woman: The Adriatic? You mean the Mediterranean?

Paul: *(impatiently)* Whatever you call it now — that stretch of open sea between Greece and Sicily. On the 15th night, I heard breakers —

Woman: The surf crashing?

Paul: Yes. And I heard the stern anchors rattle down.

Woman: Then the anchors from the bow?

Paul: They wouldn't release. And the bow swung wildly. Then I saw some of the crew dropping the long-boat.

Woman: Deserting?

Paul: It looked that way, though they said they intended to loosen the bow anchors. I alerted Julius. His soldiers hacked loose the long-boat.

Woman: So — it was to be all saved or no one saved. The stern anchors held?

Paul: Through a long anxious night. As the darkness changed to gray, I gathered everyone together. God had shown me we would all be saved. I told them that — and I made them eat —

Woman: When daylight came, could you tell where you were?

Paul: No. But we could see a bay on a rocky island.

Woman: What was the plan?

Paul: The captain ordered the men to rig up the mainsail, draw in the anchors, unlash the paddles and drive for the beach.

Woman: He planned to run aground?

Paul: It was all he could do. When the boat hit the sand, it stuck fast, its bow high in the air. The surf broke open the stern.

Woman: What a wild scramble there must have been!

Paul: My, yes. The soldiers drew their swords to kill the prisoners.

Woman: Why?

Paul: It was customary. If a prisoner escaped, his guard had to undergo his sentence and penalty. But Julius stopped the soldiers.

Woman: Because of you?

Paul: Possibly. Julius ordered all who could swim to jump overboard, those on the bow to slide down planks to the beach. And all others to grab a piece of the stern and float in on the waves.

Woman: You all got off?

Paul: Every single one. As God had promised, all came safely to land.

Woman: And what land did you find it to be?

Paul: The island of Malta, just south of Sicily. The natives of Malta came running to help us — they built fires along the beach.

Woman: Everyone stretched out to rest and to get dry, I suppose?

Paul: Some. I was so glad to feel firm ground under my feet I walked around gathering up brushwood. And when I threw some on the fire, a snake fastened onto my arm.

Woman: A poisonous snake?

Paul: The people of Malta thought so! They stood around waiting for me to swell up and die! I shook the snake into the fire.

Woman: They must have thought you had extraordinary powers.

Paul: *(laughing)* Yes, indeed! Publius, their chief, brought his sick father to me. And when Luke and I were able to help him, more people came. Luke and I ran a medical clinic for three months!

Woman: Three months? Winter would have been about over.

Paul: *(nodding)* Hmm. In March, we left on another Alexandrian ship that had wintered in Malta.

Woman: And how was your spring voyage?

Paul: Uneventful! We sailed without further trouble — landing at Syracuse on the island of Sicily and then at Rhegium in Italy —

109

Woman: Oh yes — on the tip of the boot.

Paul: We made our last stop at Puteoli.

Woman: I don't know that seaport —

Paul: A few miles west of Naples.

Woman: Oh yes, yes. It's called Puzzuoli now. You were still well more than 100 miles from Rome.

Paul: About 125. But the Christians at Puteoli made us welcome. Indeed, they pampered us for seven days!

Woman: And how did you go to Rome? Up the coastal road?

Paul: Yes. And you know *(pause, voice breaks)* — at the Apii Forum —

Woman: What, Paul?

Paul: *(close to tears)* I — I — I was met by Christians from Rome. They had marched 40 miles out the Appian Way to greet me!

Woman: Wonderful!

Paul: Overwhelming — overwhelming.

Woman: Tell me, Paul, how was it there were Christians in Italy?

Paul: The Gospel had traveled to Rome from the great cities of Asia and of eastern Europe.

Woman: Cities where you had preached —

Paul: And Christians, including Priscilla and Aquila from Ephesus, had come back to Rome.

Woman: Oh? When?

Paul: When it was safe — after the Emperor Claudius had died.

Woman: Did you enter Rome through the Porta Capena?

Paul: Yes — on a lovely early summer day.

Woman: And walked past the Circus Maximus?

Paul: *(nodding)* Hmmm. And above it, I saw the Palatine hill where Nero's palace stood. And the large open forum above the Capitoline hill — and at its foot the stone from which all roads in the empire were measured.

Woman: Roads you had traveled, Paul.

Paul: *(slowly)* All my roads that had led, at last, to Rome.

Woman: How were you received by the Roman authorities, Paul?

Paul: With the utmost consideration — due to Julius, I believe.

Woman: I'm sure he told the authorities about your saving the soldiers' lives at Malta.

Paul: Possibly. At any rate, I was placed under house arrest.

Woman: What does house arrest mean?

Paul: I was permitted to rent my own house, to receive visitors, and to walk about. Of course, I had a Roman guard — a different one every night. Often we talked for hours.

Woman: And so the Gospel spread through the Roman Praetorium! And what about the Jews in Rome?

Paul: The first thing I did was to call my people to my house.

Woman: You never gave up on the Jews, did you Paul?

Paul: How could I? I taught the Gospel to the Jews, but most would not believe. I tell you *(emotionally)* I could scarcely bear the tragedy — my people rejecting the Christ.

Woman: *(slowly)* They shut the door themselves, Paul.

Paul: Yes, and that door opened to the Gentiles. But I loved the Jews. I hung onto the comfort that there was but one Shepherd. And someday, there would be — surely — but one flock.

Woman: Were you lonely, Paul?

111

Paul: Not for the two years of house arrest! I had many visitors!

Woman: Who came?

Paul: Tychicus came from Ephesus, Demas from Thessalonica, Epaphroditus from Philippi. And my Timothy came many times.

Woman: I remember — he brought your cloak. Any others?

Paul: Onesimus, a slave who belonged to Philemon — a Christian at Colossae.

Woman: Onesimus — a runaway?

Paul: A runaway slave — but my beloved friend.

Woman: Did he stay with you?

Paul: I would like to have kept him with me. But he had to go back to Philemon.

Woman: Was that good? Wouldn't Philemon punish him?

Paul: I didn't think so. I sent a letter back with Onesimus, commending them to each other as brothers in Christ. *(pause)* And I had another visitor.

Woman: Who?

Paul: John Mark!

Woman: I presume Mark had changed a lot from that scared boy who ran back home on your first missionary journey.

Paul: *(thoughtfully)* We both had changed a lot. I had grown in understanding and compassion. Mark — Mark had grown into a fine, useful man. *(pause)* In Christ, no man nor woman need stay the way they were.

Woman: I'm glad you made peace with John Mark. You know, Paul, I had almost forgotten why you were in Rome! When did the prosecuting party from Jerusalem appear?

Paul: They never came.

Woman: Never came! Why not?

Paul: Conditions had worsened in Judea — open warfare between Jews and Romans — and — unfortunately — growing hostility between Jews and Christians. The Sanhedrin had its hands too full in Jerusalem to bother about me.

Woman: But what about Festus?

Paul: He died the year after I left Caesarea — in 62.

Woman: Then, after two years when no prosecutors had showed up —

Paul: My case just — well, disappeared. I hoped to go to Spain. But — it was not to be —

Woman: What happened?

Paul: On June 18, in 64, a fire broke out in the Circus Maximus. Fed by a high wind, flames raged through Rome for five days.

Woman: An accident?

Paul: Arson — and the people suspected Nero —

Woman: Nero? Why would Nero set fire to his own city?

Paul: He had a plan — to tear everything down — to rebuild Rome — but he was bitterly opposed.

Woman: And the people thought he burned the city down deliberately?

Paul: When word leaked out of the palace — they were sure.

Woman: But Paul — why couldn't you go to Spain? You had nothing to do with the fire —

Paul: Of course not. But Nero was in deep trouble. He needed scapegoats — and so he began a fearful persecution of the Christians. How could I leave?

Woman: I've read stories of Christians wrapped in animal skins and tossed to wild beasts in the arena.

Paul: *(sighing)* And some became human torches to light Nero's garden. Terrible, terrible —

113

Woman: And you, Paul?

Paul: Nero couldn't risk my being a rallying point for the Christians. I was arrested again — but not house arrest!

Woman: You mean — prison?

Paul: *(nodding)* Hmm. A bad one —

Woman: Did your friends help? What about Priscilla and Aquila?

Paul: I had sent them back to work at Ephesus with Timothy. And Demas —

Woman: Demas helped you?

Paul: *(short laugh)* Demas deserted me and hurried off home to Thessalonica. Only Luke stayed with me to the end.

Woman: Paul, an early Christian writer, Tertullian, compares your death with that of John the Baptist.

Paul: I would be glad to be counted among those who died for their faith — John the Baptist, many disciples — James —

Woman: Stephen —

Paul: *(sighing)* Yes, God forgive me — Stephen.

Woman: How did you spend your last days in prison, Paul?

Paul: Tying up loose ends — I appointed Titus to the church at Crete. I had already sent Timothy to Ephesus as I told you.

Woman: You felt younger men should take on your work?

Paul: It was time. My life was coming to an end. In prison, I wrote letters to both Titus and Timothy.

Woman: You wrote down those things you wished them to remember?

Paul: Oh yes. I wanted them to know how to behave — how to conduct themselves in the church — how to recognize false teachers —

Woman: Very practical.

Paul: And very important! The pastor must care for his flock, love his sheep as well. *(a rush of feeling)* The Christians were so vulnerable!

Woman: *(slowly)* They still are, Paul.

Paul: To withstand the drag of the world — in my day and in yours — men and women and boys and girls need faith in the risen Christ.

Woman: That faith which we hang onto — in our dark days.

Paul: That faith which I clung to — in my own dark days. *(pause)* And I admonished Timothy to preach that faith — that good news — to all his world.

Woman: As you had preached the Gospel to all your world! *(eagerly)* Think, Paul — in less than 40 years after the cross had been lifted on Calvary —

Paul: The Gospel had taken root —

Woman: Men and women were being set free from sin —

Paul: Free from anxiety —

Woman: Free from the law —

Paul: Free from geographical boundaries —

Woman: And free from all chains —

Paul: *(slowly)* And now — the time of my departure had come. I was free to die!

Woman: Paul *(earnestly)* You had kept the faith; you had fought the good fight —

Paul: *(slowly)* And had, at last, finished the course.

Woman: *(slowly)* Thank you, Paul, for sharing your life with us.

www.ingramcontent.com/pod-product-compliance
Lightning Source LLC
LaVergne TN
LVHW051656080426
835511LV00017B/2597